NORTH KOREAN REFORM
Politics, economics and security

ROBERT L. CARLIN AND JOEL S. WIT

ADELPHI PAPER 382

The International Institute for Strategic Studies

Arundel House | 13–15 Arundel Street | Temple Place | London | WC2R 3DX | UK

ADELPHI PAPER 382

First published July 2006 by **Routledge**
4 Park Square, Milton Park, Abingdon, Oxon, OX14 4RN

for **The International Institute for Strategic Studies**
Arundel House, 13–15 Arundel Street, Temple Place, London, WC2R 3DX, UK
www.iiss.org

Simultaneously published in the USA and Canada by **Routledge**
270 Madison Ave., New York, NY 10016

Routledge is an imprint of Taylor & Francis, an Informa business

© 2006 The International Institute for Strategic Studies

DIRECTOR-GENERAL AND CHIEF EXECUTIVE John Chipman
EDITOR Tim Huxley
MANAGER FOR EDITORIAL SERVICES Ayse Abdullah
ASSISTANT EDITOR Jessica Delaney
PRODUCTION Jesse Simon
COVER IMAGE Getty Images

PRINTED AND BOUND IN GREAT BRITAIN BY Bell & Bain Ltd, Thornliebank, Glasgow

British Library Cataloguing in Publication Data
A catalogue record for this book is available from the British Library

Library of Congress Cataloguing in Publication Data

ISBN 0-415-40725-7
ISSN 0567-932X

Contents

CHRONOLOGY OF MAJOR ECONOMIC AND NUCLEAR DEVELOPMENTS

Jan. 2001	Kim Jong Il visits China
Jul. 2002	Reform package launched with 'economic management improvement measures'
Sept. 2002	Beginning of expansion of special economic zones in Shineuiju, Gaeseong and Mt Geumgang
Oct. 2002	US Assistant Secretary of State James Kelly visits Pyongyang
Nov. 2002	Korea Peninsula Energy Development Organisation decision to halt heavy fuel-oil deliveries
Dec. 2002	Democratic People's Republic of Korea (DPRK) breaks seals at Yongbyon; IAEA inspectors withdraw
Jan. 2003	DPRK withdraws from the Nuclear Non-Proliferation Treaty
Feb. 2003	DPRK restarts five-megawatt reactor at Yongbyon
Mar. 2003	Reform in commercial establishment of general markets and authorisation of private commercial activities. Ultimate goal of enterprises adjusted to 'increase in net profit'
Apr. 2003	DPRK announcement on reprocessing
Jan. 2004	Reforms in agricultural and enterprise sectors including introduction of 'family-unit farming system' with autonomous farming
Apr. 2004	Kim Jong Il visits China. DPRK prime minister inspects pilot village for agricultural reforms
Feb. 2005	DPRK announcement on possession of nuclear weapons
May 2005	DPRK announcement on unloading five-megawatt reactor
Nov. 2005	Joint ventures allowed more domestic access and to hold profits in foreign exchange
Jan. 2006	Kim Jong Il visits China

INTRODUCTION

In recent years, analysis concerning the Democratic People's Republic of Korea (DPRK), or North Korea, has focused primarily on whether it has nuclear weapons or whether it has embarked on a programme of 'real' economic reform. There is a vague sense that the two issues may be linked in some way, a linkage usually assumed to take the form of nuclear 'chips' the North Koreans may choose to play at the negotiating table, trading them for economic benefits. For the purposes of understanding the diplomatic process, this notion of trade-offs might be a useful starting point. For understanding the larger dynamics underway in the North Korean leadership over the past several years, it is a dead end.

There are indeed links between the North's security and economic policies, but these are being reconsidered in Pyongyang as part of a larger debate in the leadership that has already transformed the country in fundamental ways. For decades, the most powerful voices in Pyongyang argued that North Korea had to resolve a number of external problems before changing its basic domestic economic policies. Security concerns always trumped economic ideas. This approach changed in late 2001. At present, no one outside the leadership circles in Pyongyang knows why, although a good guess is that Kim Jong Il simply ran out of patience. The North Korean leader had long been awaiting a decisive improvement in relations with the United States before launching economic reform measures. He probably thought he had achieved this goal by late 2000, after an exchange of high-level visits by US and DPRK officials. But then relations stalled and began moving backwards with the new administration, and by autumn 2001 he decided he would wait no more. He did not take this decision lightly. Kim Jong Il had suggested to foreigners on several occasions that he was concerned with how difficult it was to introduce new ideas into the North Korean system. He turned out to be right.

In many respects, what is playing out today in the North Korean leadership is no different from the long-term friction that occurs when any government's domestic and foreign policies rub against each other. To a certain extent, this has been going on in Pyongyang since the DPRK's founding in 1948, though usually at a level and in a way difficult for outsiders to discern. And although this correlation between internal and external policies may be well understood by the players in Pyongyang, it has been baffling to outsiders. Generally, the best that observers could do was to sense a vague consistency between these two aspects of policy.

Real or imagined, this consistency appeared to correlate with a number of well-worn assumptions about how nations respond under stress. These generally run as follows: when a country feels threatened, it tightens up domestically; political considerations override economic decisions; experimentation gives way to regimentation; and ideological discipline – or put another way, orthodoxy – takes the front seat. By the same token, the recipe for economic reform seems to require substantial external stability. Taking economic steps that risk loosening central political control is rarely seen as an option for regimes under external threat. Thus, a government will seek to put its external security in order before turning to domestic problems. Equally, debates on domestic issues often spill over into the foreign policy arena. Jockeying elements in the leadership seek to strengthen their positions by demonstrating their nationalist credentials, which sometimes translates into unusually tough stands on international issues.

Events in North Korea between 1960 and 2000 seem to reinforce the traditional proposition that governments tend to place security ahead of economic concerns. Pyongyang could always find good excuses for putting off major changes to its domestic economic policies. Sometimes the excuses were couched in terms of worry about the external security situation, concern about the impact of changes in its basic economic approach on re-unification with South Korea, or fretfulness about the combination of ideological and geopolitical consequences for the North of the Sino-Soviet split. In particular, efforts by some in the leadership to devote more resources to the civilian sector and the 'consumption' side of the economy were constantly overridden by those who argued for continued or even increased attention to military spending, 'accumulation' or investment

primarily in heavy industries, and the crucial need for 'economic independence'. That the latter was never fully achieved did not detract from the
power of its appeal and logic for North Korean leaders.

A new paradigm, perhaps

New thinking about economic policy began to emerge in 1997, even before
the country had recovered from the shock of Kim Il Sung's death three
years earlier and the subsequent collapse of the organised economy, which
saw the closure of factories, transportation and communications disrupted,
catastrophic food shortages and widespread hunger. By 1998, there were
signs that the effort to explore new economic ideas and approaches had
unusual staying power. And by early 2000, at what appears to have been a
key decision-making point, Pyongyang began moving on twin tracks in the
pursuit of economic changes that would support foreign-policy initiatives
and foreign-policy initiatives that would reinforce new economic decisions.
With the change of US administration in January 2001 and Washington's
consequent reluctance to engage the North diplomatically, Pyongyang
found itself frustrated in its efforts to keep the foreign and economic
policy tracks in synch. Progress on the diplomatic front stalled, even as
plans were being developed for new economic policies. By late 2001, Kim
Jong Il had evidently decided he could not wait for improved relations
with the United States to help to bring the two tracks back into align-
ment. Internally, he signalled his approval of 'profits' as a guiding theme,
establishing a new basis for economic activity at all levels. Externally, he
moved to bolster relations with South Korea, Japan, Russia, China and the
European Union. Success in these efforts, he may have calculated, would
not only improve the external situation but also directly feed into plans for
economic reform, to be launched sometime in 2002.

The formal launch came in July 2002, when Pyongyang initiated what
its officials have depicted as the most sweeping changes to the North
Korean economy since 1948. These changes have included increasing official prices and wages almost to black-market levels, devaluating the North
Korean won, increasing the amount of farmland that individuals can work
for their own profit, officially recognising informal markets (or, in the
regime's parlance, 'making space' for the market in the socialist economy),
and increasingly placing a greater range of managerial decisions for industry and agriculture in the hands of local production units. These steps and
others were designed to encourage the gradual – and controlled – growth
of market forces and incipient entrepreneurialism. They are noteworthy
in themselves, but their timing is also important because they suggest

that North Korea has finally turned on its head the earlier, long-practiced approach of letting security concerns trump economic ones. This came as a surprise to many outside observers who questioned early reports of economic reform in the North, because they regarded it as a country that considered itself to be under siege and the regime as one that would never undertake measures that would threaten its hold on power.

By early 2006, the reform process had been sustained for nearly four years, even surviving the most serious period of tensions in the bilateral relationship with the US in a decade. One good working hypothesis to account for this is that Kim Jong Il moved ahead with new economic measures in the expectation that the diplomatic and economic tracks, rather than being in tension with one another, would be mutually rein-forcing.[1] Such a decision would not have made any sense if the notion of economic reform had just fallen on his head like Newton's apple. It would be logical, however, if – as the evidence suggests – he and at least some in his circle had been examining, debating and working towards such new measures for several years. By instituting new economic measures when he did – before the external situation was resolved – Kim Jong Il set off a vigorous internal debate over the pace and scope of economic reforms and regime priorities, a debate that has gone considerably further than most outsider observers imagine.

There is little evidence to clarify which players in Pyongyang stand where on the issue of economic reform. In all likelihood, none of the iden-tifiable power centres (party, government, military, security services, for example) are monolithic. Moreover, the shifting of alignments according to individual issues is consistent with the nature of bureaucracies. Even individual players may change sides. As a result, those who consider themselves pragmatic reformers today may appear to be conservative tomorrow. The idea that, on a question like economic reform, nobody matters in Pyongyang but Kim Jong Il is almost certainly wrong. Ideas do bubble up to the top, especially where economic questions are concerned. Kim Jong Il seems predisposed to considering new thinking while sensing the danger of moving too far ahead of the old guard. He is not a first-generation revolutionary leader and has always seemed impatient with established ways of doing things, especially when it comes to the tradi-tional ideas of the Korean Workers' Party on social and economic issues. However, like his father before him, he keeps on top of problems not always by solving them, but sometimes by maintaining an ambiguous stance. Even after he makes a decision, there appears to be surprising room for continued, albeit carefully phrased, discussion.

Any rearrangement of the links between domestic and foreign policy necessarily raises important questions about how the reform process might evolve in North Korea, whether Pyongyang anticipates changes in its security and foreign policy options, and how developments on the economic front may reveal new possibilities for the outside world in dealing with North Korea on a range of issues. There have long been indications of elements in Pyongyang looking for ways to change economic priorities by taking resources from the defence sector and putting them to work more productively. Any economic reform programme in North Korea will sooner or later have to wrestle with this issue because the country's heavy military burden is a barrier not just to reform but even to economic recovery.

In the North Korean context, the situation appears complicated by the division of overall economic activity into several realms or circles. It is commonly accepted that there exist in the North several parallel – and, in some cases, overlapping – circles of economic activity. One can interpret the picture in various ways, but essentially, in addition to the socialist command economy that consists of production in state factories and on state and collective farms, there are two other elements:

- A 'second economy' serves the production of goods and services to maintain the North's huge military establishment, including over one million armed forces personnel, a significant research and development programme for weapons of mass destruction as well as conventional weapons, and a large defence-industrial base able to support such activities. Estimates vary for the size of North Korea's defence industry and its relationship to the overall economy but, by most accounts, it is significant. One recent South Korean publication claims that the defence industry accounts for 50% of the economy and 30% of national production (more than in the Soviet Union where it accounted for only 8%), surpassing the production of civilian enterprises.[2] A RAND Corporation study estimates that military spending per active North Korean military personnel is between US\$3,900 and US\$5,500 while the national product for non-military personnel is between US\$509 and US\$707, which is extraordinarily high when compared to other countries.[3]

- A third, much smaller, economic realm handles special goods and services exclusively for the use of the leadership and supports approximately three million beneficiaries at the top of the North Korean political, military and technical elites. Described by some experts as a 'court economy', Kim Jong Il and the top leadership have their own retail outlets, foreign trade organisation, as well as financial and industrial companies, which secure state resources but are unaccountable to the economic bureaucracy. These companies manufacture goods for export, the trading companies market them and profits are deposited in the financial institutions. Some of the activities of this court economy appear to include counterfeiting, drugs production and smuggling.[4]

An initial division of available resources – raw materials, labour, funds – must be made between these separate economies and another cut must be made within the circles themselves. For economic reform measures to have an impact, they must eventually deal with inequities not only within the circles but, more importantly, between them. Although the specific reform measures under discussion appear to many outside observers to be either minor or insufficient – mere tinkering with resource allocations within each circle – the crux of the debate in the North lies in the larger question of the apportionment of resources *between* the circles. Constant trumpeting of 'military first' policies in the media has tended to distract even close observers of North Korea, hiding the important subtext in these pronouncements.

Implications and imponderables

It could be that Pyongyang believes it can have both economic reform and an active nuclear weapons programme. Moreover, the dynamics in the leadership may initally push Pyongyang to try to achieve both of these goals. It would be a mistake, however, to assume that the nuclear programme is necessarily the leadership's central focus or that it takes priority over short- or long-term calculations of economic recovery. The longer the reform programme lasts and the wider it spreads through the economy, the more likely it is that contradictions in the leadership will sharpen, with not just the nuclear weapons programme but the wider issue of military spending becoming a key bone of contention.

A clean and simple outcome would be for forward movement in economic policy to affect the North's diplomatic and security policies in positive ways, and for steps towards the resolution of overarching security problems then to reinforce further development of economic reform. Equally plausible, at least at this point, however, is the possibility that the leadership will not be able to overcome the most difficult barriers to fundamental reform and that a partially reformed system will breed increasing dissatisfaction at all levels of society, leading to internal tensions, foreign policy lurches and a retreat into shrill, brittle ideological fundamentalism. Another possibility is that the struggle between pro-reform and anti-reform elements will spill over into foreign policy, with anti-reform advocates seeking to take advantage of (or even to create) increased tensions in order to assert that a hostile external environment makes reforms not only dangerous but potentially suicidal.

A note on methodology

Much of this paper is based on analysis of publicly available North Korean media sources. These can be used well or abused, depending on whether the approach taken is systematic or haphazard. Reading through the North's media and picking quotes at random would not constitute analysis. Much of what appears in the press is simply routine-level propaganda – something that is not unimportant but is nevertheless a narrow, sometimes clouded, window compared to that provided by authoritative comment.

When looking at economic reforms, the analytical difficulties are increased because little in the available commentary appears to address directly the particular reforms that are currently being implemented. There have been references in the North Korean media to wages and a few to prices, but discussions of markets and inflation are wrapped in critical analysis about capitalist practices. For the most part, reformers and conservatives alike have been forced to cloak their differences in the guise of convoluted discussions about the relative significance of defence, heavy and light industries. When they want to make major points they may cast the battle in familiar but well-understood terminology, pitting accumulation against consumption. Interpreting the meaning of these various formulations and shadings in emphasis is tricky but not impossible. Sometimes what is not said is as important as what appears in print. On occasion, the revival of an old theme is significant, not because the theme itself is crucial but because it points back to previous circumstances and decisions.

The debates reflected in the North Korean media commentary are real, but the commentaries themselves are usually only snippets, not the conversation itself, and certainly not the conversation in its entirety. For example, the sudden appearance from January 2003 of a spate of articles in the party newspaper *Nodong Sinmun* seeking to justify priority spending on the defence industry on economic rather than military grounds suggests that another conversation is going on elsewhere within the policy arena, one in which someone in the leadership is strongly – and effectively – pressing the case that defence spending is no longer a sacred cow and that its utility must be explained in economic terms.

This type of exegesis may provoke protest from those who find that a close reading of the North Korean media is tedious. But the objective is to understand this public commentary in the proper context – that is, the context in which it was written. Discussions in the controlled media are valuable precisely because they are controlled. That the discussions take place within a carefully constrained environment does not diminish their utility. It just requires a special lens to see clearly what is going on.

To avoid having to repeat countless times 'emphasis added' throughout the paper, we have italicised those words or phrases that seem to us (and, more to the point, were probably meant to be) particularly important in the media articles we quote. In some cases, the relevant articles are quoted at length, because they reflect real differences in the leadership over important policy options. In presenting the documentary evidence we faced a difficult problem in deciding on an organising principle. Although a few themes are coming to the fore in the media debate over reform, there are not yet enough to provide a reasonable thematic basis for discussion. At this stage, the most practical approach seems to be chronological. That has given the presentation something of the flavour of a tennis match, as we trace the arguments bouncing back and forth between those whom, in somewhat simplified terms, we have labelled conservatives and reformers.

CHAPTER ONE

Debate and Policy Formation

The very idea of debate in Pyongyang strikes many observers as implausible. However, it should come as no surprise that even within the North Korean leadership there are differences of opinion, sometimes merely over questions of tactics, but at other times over more fundamental issues. Not all decisions are equally open to question and, even for those decisions on which there can be differences, there may only be limited opportunities for expressing opposing points of view.

To this degree, the term 'policy debate' may be somewhat misleading. In the North Korean context, it should not conjure up images of full-throated, openly voiced policy differences. When differences are expressed in the leadership, they tend to be argued within fairly narrow and well-understood boundaries. While it is possible to speak up against taking a specific step, it is not prudent to question the basic leadership decision that is the foundation for the particular measure in question, for that would come too close to questioning the leader himself, perhaps with unhappy consequences. It may be more accurate, therefore, to speak of differences of approach as a function of different – and contending – schools of thought within the leadership. Even after a 'decision' has been made, various groups are still free to emphasise different shadings of interpretation. What is remarkable about the differences over economic reform since early 2002 is that the shadings have been considerably less nuanced than usual. In some cases, they have been as subtle as black and white.

Debate is a notion many observers have a hard time fitting to North Korea because they tend to assume that the country's policies emerge suddenly, apparently from no clear source, and that the impulses driving major decisions in other countries are strangely absent from Pyongyang. On the contrary, while the timing for implementation may be whimsical and unpredictable, long periods of discussion and preparation are typical of the North's approach to trying out new ideas. Its policies rarely reverse course sharply, nor do they lurch with every change in political line. In fact, North Korea's policy-making (as opposed to its rhetoric) is cautious, as befits a small, weak power unsure of its next step and fearful of what might lie ahead. Long periods of experimentation are the norm, probably both to ensure that the process works and to dampen the possibilities of criticism for costly blunders.

Thus, it is not surprising that, from the beginning, there were strong indications that the first steps in the recent economic reforms were in some sense experimental. During such periods of experimentation, there is often a parallel period of debate over exactly how to interpret and carry out policy guidelines. Despite stark differences of approach, as far as can be discerned, the debate that came to the fore in 2002 (or even earlier) has been conducted largely within boundaries that are recognised and apparently accepted. There is no reason to suppose that any policy-maker in Pyongyang wanted an unending series of spontaneous, extra-legal developments to continue in the economy. Economic officials of all stripes, reformers and non-reformers alike, would want to see the economy as a whole developing in what they considered to be a rational, balanced and planned fashion. The issue, therefore, was not a two-dimensional dispute over 'free markets' versus 'state planning', but over how to accomplish that goal. Significant differences have emerged over allocating resources, setting priorities and fashioning means by which to encourage economic activity to generate revenue and to keep the population reasonably content.

Obviously, this quest was not simply one of theoretical economics. Depending on whose views prevailed, there would inevitably be winners and losers in the general population and, perhaps more importantly, in the elite. Some would gain power, others lose it. There are broad ideological issues at stake and huge national security concerns involved. No North Korean official would argue for weakening the country's defences, not only for fear of being called a traitor, but also because none would believe it to be a wise course. But the question of how much defence is enough under present circumstances is not easy to answer. In fact, it is one of the most sensitive and contentious problems along the reform path. When asked, North Korean officials tell outsiders that they see no contradiction between the demands of economic reforms and defence. Perhaps some do not genuinely see any such contradiction, but others apparently do. They have written frequently and at length on the question. What to do about the military's role in the midst of economic reforms quickly became a central issue for discussion once the reforms were launched. There is as yet no sign that the issue has been resolved, and therein lies the most interesting part of the tale.

The conservative approach, with its arguments couched in terms of the importance of the military first slogan, is most obvious in the appearance of a number of *Nodong Sinmun* editorial board special articles since 2002. In each case, these articles take up the entire first page of the party newspaper, sometimes more. They unmistakably trumpet their own importance and tend to be highly orthodox. But, surprisingly, they do not represent the last word. Instead, they appear to have been the first blasts and then bleats of protest from conservatives who, judging by the evolution of the arguments in these pieces, have been forced to beat a slow retreat into accepting an uneasy coexistence with the new economic measures.

The other side, representing the impulse towards change and frequently an implicit challenge to orthodox interpretations of the military first concept, is in evidence fairly consistently in the quarterly economic journal, *Kyongje Yongu*, a publication that is not necessarily the leading edge of reformist thinking or its authoritative mouthpiece, but more often than not seems to reflect quite accurately reformist currents in policy-level discussions. Not every article is equally daring, some being relatively orthodox in their approach, but overall the journal seems to march to the beat of a reformist drum. Significantly, the journal did not give prominent attention to the military first idea until its August 2003 volume, more than a year after the topic became a central, almost daily focus in newspapers and speeches.

The premier and the cabinet, in charge of not merely implementing, but also developing economic reform, draw on bodies of scholars and economists who are writing and debating the question of new economic policies. There have been hints that university journals have been used as a channel for expressing and circulating new ideas.[1] These may or may not be linked directly with what appears in *Kyongje Yongu*. It is possible that the party journal *Kulloja* is also a forum for leading discussion, but it has not been available to outsiders for several years. Judging from the conservative bent of several joint *Nodong Sinmun–Kulloja* articles that Pyongyang has publicised, however, it appears likely that *Kulloja* is not a voice for reform and instead remains a hilltop fortress for those who would prefer to keep the reforms at bay.

Judging from the number of articles in the media, there has been and continues to be considerable internal discussion about the reforms. There has been too much debate sustained over many years for the reforms to be merely a charade. The continuing discussion does not indicate which side will eventually come out on top, but the fact that the reforms are still in place and that reformers continue to make their case lends weight to the conclusion that, while policy-makers in the North may still have numerous questions about how and when to move forward, it is apparent that they are already well down the road towards implementing new economic policies.

Currently, we do not know whether or to what extent internal security measures have been altered to accommodate the new economic policies, although on the surface there appear to have been adjustments. A to-and-fro dance on the issue of mobile phones continues and indicates the degree to which old boundaries are no longer sacred. The security services were forced to accept a decision in 2003 (probably by Kim Jong Il) to allow wider mobile-phone usage. They were able to restrict usage again in 2004, but the game is hardly over. Even the growth in the past five years of an intranet linking people – largely students and officials – in widely separated parts of the country poses risks that may seem unacceptable to those in charge of internal security. Security concerns may weigh heavily in North Korean calculations, but they do not always rule the roost. A 1996 decision to allow regular passenger runs by a South Korean ship up the DPRK's east coast – to carry workers on the construction project conducted by the Korean Peninsula Energy Development Organization (KEDO) – overcame internal opposition, presumably from the navy. Pyongyang's consent in 1998 to over-flights by foreign air carriers in exchange for fees appears to have represented a decision by Kim Jong Il to put aside long-standing security objections. And the British government finally won permission in 2003 for its embassy to operate secure satellite communications after what was apparently strong advice to North Korea's government from its security services to the contrary.

The cabinet and especially the premier have been given a higher public profile in the past few years. This is not only consistent with their task of operationalising the reforms, but also serves to emphasise the continuing legitimacy of the reforms themselves. Reports in the media on cabinet plenums, which take place several times throughout the year, barely give a nod to military first priorities and devote noticeably more attention to issues of management reform. It would be going too far to say that the premier and the cabinet have become a new power centre, let alone independent actors. Their role in developing and refining economic policies undoubtedly takes place within fairly well-understood parameters. At the level of the ministries themselves, there is little evidence so far of how they feed into the reform process. Specific ministries appear to be playing a supporting role, though perhaps as much out of self-interest as in pursuit of lofty policy goals. The foreign trade ministry, for example, has an interest in reforms especially to the extent that these enhance its importance. Similarly, a number of committees and newly formed organs designed to interact with the outside world appear to be playing a dual role as salesman and conduit for the ideas and experience necessary to bolster and sustain the reforms. The foreign ministry does not appear central to either the decision–making on or implementation of the reforms, but ultimately its role is crucial in creating the external environment necessary for their success. However, the extent to which this task is considered central to the foreign ministry's calculations is an open question.

CHAPTER TWO

The Way Things Were

Within North Korea, decisions about the economy have always been intensely political. They were intertwined with ideological discourse in the communist world, woven into the fabric of the Sino-Soviet confrontation (which Pyongyang could not ignore and to which it had to respond) and connected to internal arguments over national independence versus integration into larger, primarily Soviet-bloc economic systems. Before the Sixth Workers' Party Congress of October 1980 introduced a sweeping new concept of re-unification, there was great concern that the wrong economic policies might adversely affect prospects for unification – both in terms of the 'influence' they might have on South Koreans and on preparations for the 'great day'. Some economic decisions were justified on the grounds that devoting resources to a particular sector was unnecessary because, after the liberation of the South, more than enough resources would be available to go around. A good deal of these justifications were no doubt propaganda, but some of them may equally have amounted to self-delusion.

Put another way, North Korean economic policies have not emerged from a political vacuum, but from leadership decisions after discussions of neither a theoretical nor an academic nature. Certainly, after the Korean War (1950–53), North Korean economic policies were the butt of criticism from East European communists who saw them as badly conceived and poorly executed. Frequently, the embassies of these countries were only slightly better informed than the common observer and their reporting carried a heavy dose of personal bias, mixed with elements of pique and boredom. It is hard to find communist observers who did not sneer at North Korean economic decisions.[1] Yet the interesting question, then as now, is not what the policies were, but how they came to be decided on in the first place.

Eastern bloc embassies in Pyongyang were full of advice for the regime on how to run its economy. How much of this was actually transmitted to the North Korean leadership in a manner it might take on board and how much was simply communicated back to capitals in the form of wry observations from frustrated diplomats serving out their Korean postings remains unclear. From the available collections of Soviet-bloc diplomatic traffic, it appears that some communist diplomats made an effort, which in some cases was rather heavy handed, to lecture North Korean officials on what they were doing wrong. Then, as now, North Korean bureaucrats did not take kindly to being told by foreigners how to run their affairs. Nevertheless, in some cases it looks as if the advice did strike a chord. The North Koreans certainly followed developments in 'fraternal' countries and appeared aware of – and recognised the need to adjust to – many of the debates about economic policy that were underway in Moscow, Eastern European capitals and Beijing.

The diplomatic correspondence suggests that on several occasions in the 1950s and 1960s, whether as a result of external advice or not, the leadership in Pyongyang embarked on a series of corrective measures, such as tinkering with agricultural policy, increasing investment in light industry and easing restrictions on the possession of private land or the operations of markets. These measures could not be classed as major reforms, but in the context of trying to develop a socialist society, the leadership found even these decisions ideologically sensitive and difficult to make.

Some might claim that North Korean policies and behaviour have not really changed, that they remain on the same, unshakeable vector they have been on since at least the late 1960s. On the contrary, changes in the security environment as well as changes in the leadership (especially generational changes) have significantly affected how the North Koreans see themselves and how they understand what, practically, they can hope to accomplish. It is worth underlining here that the North Koreans have always tended to favour pragmatism over ideology. This inclination was demonstrated even in the 1960s and early 1970s when they were effectively hemmed in by serious ideological disputes raging in the international communist movement. To take the example of agricultural policy, the North Koreans knew that this was a sensitive subject in the early 1960s because of how it figured in the Sino-Soviet conflict.[2] Watched closely by both Moscow and Beijing, they felt their own choices were constrained, with every step having to be explained not only in economic, but also political terms.

The situation eased somewhat in the 1980s, when reform was in the air in China, Eastern Europe and finally in the Soviet Union itself. Pyongyang paid close attention to the political and economic angles of these developments. Kim Il Sung's visits to Eastern Europe in 1984 and 1988 brought economic issues to the fore when he saw the situation abroad with his own eyes and demanded to know why the North Korean economy could not do as well. But to the extent that there were efforts to explore the applicability of the reform measures being implemented in the Soviet Union and Eastern Europe – reflected in renewed debate in Pyongyang over the importance of light industry and consumer goods and, not coincidentally, in efforts to establish a special economic zone at Najin-Sonbong, which, like similar efforts in China, could serve as a testing ground for new economic policy – these were limited by counter-arguments about the need to deal first with the external security threat from the United States and the South. During his May 1984 visit, Kim Il Sung told General Secretary of the Socialist Unity Party of East Germany Erich Hönecker:

> We have to take countermeasures every time the enemies conduct military exercises, and this is a great hindrance to our production. Since the number of soldiers in our army is smaller than that of the South Korean army, we have to mobilize many workers in these cases. *But when the workers are mobilized, one work shift is dropped for up to one and a half months per year. This is a great loss.*[3]

This lament was not just meant for Hönecker's ears; it had been a topic of discussion within the leadership for some time.

The sense of an imperative in Pyongyang for economic change was blunted but not broken by the collapse of the regimes in Eastern Europe and the Soviet Union in the late 1980s and early 1990s. The disappearance of the old export markets and sources of aid apparently opened the way on the North Korean side for economic 'realists' to play a prominent role in the inter-Korean dialogue of the early 1990s. In many ways, the resolution of the first nuclear crisis in 1994 owed much to North Korean efforts to improve their external security environment as a necessary step towards domestic economic change.

In sum, over the past 25 years, elements in the leadership have attempted to try 'new' ideas in the economic sphere. The first attempt was in the mid-1980s, following the resolutions of the Sixth Workers' Party Congress and coinciding with the development of a more accommodating line towards South Korea. The second was in the early 1990s, when there was not only a push towards establishing a dialogue with Seoul, but also with the United States. Neither of these efforts was ever really reversed, both simply petered out when negative events overtook them. The first could not be sustained in the midst of the shock caused to the North's economy by the collapse of the Soviet Union. The second disappeared in the near-collapse of the economy and fraying of the political structure that followed Kim Il Sung's death in 1994.

Often, the individuals leading these economic efforts – who are usually in the second tier of the leadership – do not appear to have fared well, though it is not clear whether the problem has been primarily the policies they advocated or the sharp edges of their personalities. A notable example is former Vice Premier Kim Dal Hyon, a key figure in pushing new economic ideas from 1991 to 1993 before his demotion.[4] Indeed, personalities often appear to be as important as ideology in Pyongyang; individuals on the same side of the ideological divide are often bitter enemies and, for personal reasons, attack each other in ways that ultimately hurt the positions they jointly advocate. Pushing new ideas is a good way to establish a higher profile, but a higher profile sets one up as a target for personal – as well as bureaucratic and ideological – enemies.

Operating assumptions

In considering the evolution of the economic reform process that began in North Korea in 2001–02, this paper makes a number of reasoned assumptions. First, by the 1980s, important segments of the North Korean leadership knew that their economy had lost the race with South Korea, and worse, that it was no longer performing according to the expectations of the leadership. Second, by the early 1990s, the top leadership had concluded that North Korea's traditional alliances were dead and that accommodation with the United States was crucial. Finally, by 2000, the 'realists' in the leadership had no doubt in their minds that without substantial and immediate changes in domestic policies, the regime and perhaps even North Korea as a country were unsustainable. No more than working assumptions, these have proved useful in predicting North Korean behaviour and, in retrospect, they help to explain the development of its policies over the past 20 years. Although it is likely that none of these are exactly right, neither are they out of character with North Korean leadership calculations, as we are beginning to understand them in light of the emerging historical record.

In this regard, it is worth noting that some officials in Pyongyang saw the 11 June 1993 US–DPRK Joint Statement, which was concluded just before

North Korea was slated to withdraw from the Nuclear Non-Proliferation Treaty (NPT), as a decisive step towards new economic policies. By promising the normalisation of relations with the United States, it provided a rationale for discarding the security driven laws and regulations previously justified by the long state of 'hostility'. The joint statement was seen (too hopefully as it turned out) not simply as a diplomatic breakthrough, but as a necessary step for finally breaking the tight control that conservatives in the leadership exerted over economic policy. At last it would be possible to justify changes to the suffocating, five-decade-old internal security arrangements that had in the past been used to trump proposals for economic reform.

The death of Kim Il Sung in 1994 and the implosion of the centrally planned North Korean economy (evident, most notably, in serious disruptions to the public distribution system) threw the country into a state of turmoil that it had not seen since the Korean War. Not surprisingly, the ensuing years of extreme economic hardship and devastating food shortages contained the seeds of change. In September 1997, Pyongyang hosted a formal fact-finding mission from the International Monetary Fund, followed by an 'introductory' mission from the World Bank five months later, reflecting a new willingness to study (though not yet to move forward with) international financial institutions and the policies they represented. By the summer of 1998, even clearer signs emerged that Kim Jong Il was opening the door to far-reaching alterations in economic policy. Changes to the North Korean constitution and the re-organisation of the government – integrating the policy-making and implementation functions of the ministries into a revamped and strengthened cabinet system – contained hints of new economic approaches that were also increasingly reflected in *Kyongje Yongu*. The journal began to overflow with articles which either read like capitalist primers or offered historical examples of profound economic change in the country from as far back as the Koryo Dynasty (918–1392). While it is unlikely that these early articles represented approved policies, it is also unlikely that they would have been written (much less published) if there were not a strong sense within the system that it was safe to push beyond old boundaries and to explore new ideas.

CHAPTER THREE

Preparation for Economic Reform

Most analysis of contemporary North Korean economic reforms focuses heavily on the particulars of specific measures, but does not investigate closely the process through which the reforms have emerged.[1] Yet, at this early stage, it is as much the process by which the new economic measures emerge as the details of the measures themselves that can tell us something about the seriousness and sustainability of the reforms launched by Kim Jong Il in July 2002. Some observers believe that there is not enough information on decision-making in Pyongyang to allow them to look at the process; others do not even believe in the existence of a 'process' in the North Korean system, but assume that the most important policies are simply handed down from the top.

In any case, no economic reform programme is simply about economic policy and that of Pyongyang is no exception. From the beginning, it has been intertwined with the on-going political struggle for power and influence in the leadership. The battles over the reforms are not short-lived affairs. They are fought over a number of years, as the various participants manoeuvre to shape critical decisions about who will control the state's scarce resources and to what end.

While there were numerous signs in the North of serious thinking about economic reform as early as the late 1990s, it was not until February 2000 that Pyongyang sent an exceptionally strong signal that economic considerations had risen in importance in the regime's list of immediate policy concerns. Using a highly unusual vehicle – reporting remarks attributed to Vice Premier Cho Chang Dok supposedly in response to a Korean Central News Agency (KCNA) reporter's questions – Pyongyang publicly asserted that the 'political, ideological and military might can be considered as having *already* reached that of a powerful state'.[2] This formulation – later attributed to Kim Jong Il himself – became perhaps the single most important banner under which the reformers could gather. Implicit, but perfectly clear in it was the assessment that sufficient emphasis had already been placed on the three central concerns – politics, ideology and the military. Now, it was time to devote more attention to the economy, and not just in the form of ideological exhortations either. 'We can also become a strong economic power within a few years', Cho Chang Dok was quoted as saying, 'if we concentrate our efforts on economic construction'.

The formulation presaged what was to become a major fault-line in the leadership, if indeed it had not already emerged as one. This was the question of finding the proper place for defence spending within overall efforts to renovate the economy by 'improving' its foundations in conformity with the 'new situation'. The claim that the country was 'already' powerful militarily became a rallying point for those advocating a break with the past practice of giving absolute priority in resource allocation to the military. This one word, 'already', stands out against the constant arguments to the contrary by conservatives that the development of military power and the defence industry should be given priority or, to use the terminology employed in these public discussions, that 'bullets' must come before 'candies'.

Cho Chang Dok's public pronouncement was followed by a series of high-level diplomatic moves designed to transform North Korea's security environment and to push reform forward. In late May 2000, Kim Jong Il made his first public trip to China in almost two decades. The Inter-Korean Summit with South Korean President Kim Dae Jung occurred one month later. In October, North Korea and the United States issued a joint communiqué after a visit to Washington by a senior military leader that seemed to place their relations on a new footing. Later that month, US Secretary of State Madeleine Albright visited Pyongyang and had several long meetings with Kim Jong Il. The visit was important in North Korean eyes because it seemed to increase the likelihood that the DPRK's external security environment would improve, clearing the way for economic reforms.

Some might argue that, if US–DPRK bilateral relations had continued to improve, this would only have relieved pressure on Pyongyang sufficiently to obviate the need for real economic change. But it is more likely that Kim Jong Il's plans for economic change were waiting for just such a transformation of the external situation, which is probably one reason why he invested himself so heavily and so publicly in the Albright visit. His next foreign relations move, another visit to China in January 2001 just as the new US administration was taking office, supports this hypothesis. Not having been to China in nearly two decades, he went twice within six months. Presumably by that point Kim Jong Il had already made the decision to move ahead with his economic reform programme; he brought along a large military–party contingent to Shanghai in January to show sceptics the fruits of reform in China. The group toured the stock exchange and a General Motors joint-venture plant. According to the Chinese foreign ministry, Kim Jong Il praised the achievements of China's economic reforms.[3] That praise was not only for his hosts; it was undoubtedly intended as a signal to DPRK officials, those who had accompanied him and those waiting in Pyongyang.

To herald the visit, the joint (i.e., party, military and youth organs) New Year editorial for 2001 had re-emphasised the key line introduced almost a year earlier, a line that ran, more than ever, against any effort by conservatives to insist on a literal interpretation of military first ideology:

> National economic power is the basis of socialist strength, prosperity and rehabilitation. The principle of socialist politics is that an invincible military power and political and ideological power *should be supported, without fail, by strong economic power.* No task is more important for us than to build up a national economic power that corresponds to the 21st century.[4]

During 2001, however, US–North Korean engagement ground to a halt, with the new US administration either indifferent or hostile to progress on the diplomatic front. North Korean officials worried aloud that conservatives, not just in Washington, but also in Pyongyang, were undermining the structure established over the preceding eight years. Internal discussions about significant economic changes appear to have proceeded nevertheless. In June 2001, visitors to Pyongyang heard economic officials claim that they were being urged to 'perfect' socialist management practices – a euphemism for the introduction of significantly new economic practices, they freely admitted. In October 2001, a year after what he had hoped would be a crucial breakthrough with Washington, Kim Jong Il finally introduced the themes that would form the philosophical underpinnings for the reform measures to follow over the next few years: profits, results and expertise.

The conservative response, an authoritative voice sounding notes of concern and caution, appeared in a rare joint *Nodong Sinmun–Kulloja* article two months later, focusing on the need to stick to military first policies. It underlined the case that emphasis on the military was not a temporary phenomenon and could not be put aside when tensions subsided – a jab at the twinned diplomatic–economic-reform effort that was gaining momentum.[5] Beyond this, though, conservatives largely held back from expressing reservations, at least in public. The first half of 2002 was a period of almost free rein for commentary pushing reform, even after US President George W. Bush's State of the Union address in January 2002, in which he designated North Korea a member of the 'axis of evil'. At the same time, the diplomatic pace picked up with a multi-pronged North Korean effort towards all points of the compass – Japan, South Korea, the European Union, China and Russia. Most important for Kim Jong Il, in terms of his schedule for implementing the first phase of reforms, was a senior-level foreign ministry meeting with the United States planned for June 2002. In Pyongyang's view, this meeting would put the process of improving relations with Washington back on track.

However, in April 2002, as the diplomatic pace accelerated, there was an ominous conservative reaction in the form of a *Nodong Sinmun* editorial board special article. The article carried further the warnings of the joint *Nodong Sinmun–Kulloja* article of the preceding December and argued: 'Politics underrating guns and ideology, and *politics dominated by money* cannot raise an army that has strong conviction and determination, even in a hundred years.' The language became even more astonishingly bold, given the scope of the North's diplomacy during those months:

> Modern revisionists at one time melted even tanks and guns that required blood and sweat to manufacture and weakened defense capabilities while crying for a peaceful coexistence lacking principle. For one to jettison the principle of giving precedence to military affairs in the era of peaceful construction when no guns of war are fired is like digging one's own grave. This eventually is surrender to the imperialists and a betrayal to the revolution.[6]

The article put those seeking to use diplomacy to help the economic reforms in its sights:

> Making a showdown with imperialism while looking at someone and hoping for someone else's assistance is the road of ruining everything ... Those who are afraid of imperialism would seek

to please the imperialists in a servile manner, making compromises and concessions without principles, and even give up the
anti-imperialist struggle.[7]

With the promulgation of the reforms three months away, the *Nodong
Sinmun* piece drew the battle-lines for a fight over basic priorities: 'Our
hard-line stance is definitely not a temporary measure to meet the trend of
the situation.' And after a requisite nod to the importance of the economy
– 'if the economy is stagnant, we will not be able to stop the imperialists' economic aggression' – the article went on to argue that, in contrast to
what the reformers contended, the economy was actually not lagging and
in any case it was not all that crucial to the struggle:

> Our economic foundation is solid … The most acute sectors in
> the confrontation with imperialists are the political and foreign
> relations sectors. Political and military strength is behind the
> diplomatic war to safeguard the country's sovereignty.[8]

Relentlessly focusing on the diplomatic question, the article emphasised:

> Success or failure of foreign relations is related to strength. A
> skillful diplomatic strategy that puts the enemies into a dilemma
> does not come from the air but from one's courage that comes
> from one's independent strength.[9]

And warning those tempted to adopt policies (presumably in the economic
sphere) that appealed to outsiders, the article said:

> Being praised by the enemy means that one deviates from the
> road of the anti-imperialist struggle. Revolutionaries who have
> stood up in the anti-imperialist struggle must be able to see
> horrific toxin from the enemy's sweet words.[10]

The July 2002 meeting with the United States never took place, ostensibly
scuppered by a clash between the North and South Korean navies off the
peninsula's west coast.[11] Yet even though progress on the diplomatic front
with the United States was key to securing a propitious external environment, Kim Jong Il was not prepared to delay economic reforms any longer.
The first phase started on 1 July and incrementally over the following few
months, far-reaching changes were implemented: wage and price increases;
adjustments in exchange rates; enhancement of autonomy in industrial
management; consolidation of the incentives system for farming; and the
near-abolishment of the rationing system.[12] In an effort to reduce the shock

and to ease the transition, teams fanned out from Pyongyang throughout the country to explain the new measures.

Conservative warnings came quickly. Two more *Nodong Sinmun* editorial board special articles appeared in July and August.[13] Both steered clear of explicitly addressing economic themes, but their warnings on diplomacy had economic barbs, probably designed with the prospect of progress in Japan–North Korean relations in mind. (Prime Minister Junichiro Koizumi visited Pyongyang in September.) The August article criticised those who would like to 'hold out their hand for outside help' on the 'pretext' of adapting to a 'new environment'. This barb was aimed at one of the primary arguments of the reform effort, that new and changing circumstances required new policies. Picking up a theme from the April editorial board article, it warned that 'foreign capital' could not be mightier than 'revolutionary spirit'. And in what looks to be an almost breathtakingly reckless charge against the reformers, the article railed against those using the theme of science and technology to 'belittle the role of the revolutionary spirit'. It drove home the point, warning:

> Confrontation with imperialists cannot be done with mathematical calculations and technological computations alone. It is the army with guns and people, not the computer that fights war.[14]

Given Kim Jong Il's personal support for science and technology, especially his interest in computers, this blast at technology was striking in the extreme.

If the reformers were cowed, they did not show it. The 20 August edition of *Kyongje Yongu* included a piece (certainly written when the *Nodong Sinmun* special article of 19 August appeared, but possibly not finished until after the earlier *Nodong Sinmun* special article of 31 July) that confronted the sensitive subject of the balance between accumulation and consumption, a concept central to considerations over how to divide the economic pie, especially in light of the reforms. The article pressed the point that, for the economy to develop and grow, 'produced products should be swiftly consumed'. And for the swift consumption of 'produced products', increases in production needed to be followed by an increase in the purchasing power of the people. The more money people had, the more consumer goods they would want; the more they bought, the more production would increase demand and drive the need for new investment in 'means of production', that is, machinery, transportation and mining. This approach fitted well with the philosophy behind the economic reforms. It did not fit at all with the concept of allocating priority to the defence industry, which the conservatives were waiting to unleash under the label of 'military first'. In fact, the article made no reference at all to the defence sector or the military.[15]

More evidence of reformist staying power appeared in mid-September 2002, in a *Nodong Sinmun* article reviewing a number of policies under Kim Il Sung, including those which called for giving priority to heavy industry while simultaneously developing light industry and agriculture, and for carrying on economic construction and defence-building in parallel.[16] The article carefully addressed the question of economic priorities. It granted that 'history shows that a country with meagre military power cannot maintain its dignity even when it has a long history and tradition and advanced economic strength'. But nowhere did it endorse the idea that developing the economy should play second fiddle to developing military power. If anything, its major theme was the need for balance:

> The fact that we build a powerful state does not mean merely that we develop our economy and raise the standards of the people's material and cultural living. Of course, building an economic power is one of our most important goals today. The target of our struggle for constructing a powerful state is fundamentally to renovate our country's general appearance in accordance with the demands of the new century.[17]

This reiteration of previous exhortations calling for balanced economic development may have been directly linked to a new line determined by Kim Jong Il, calling for the priority to be granted to the defence industry while simultaneously developing light industry and agriculture. Whatever the intent, by substituting 'defence industry' for 'heavy industry', he set up a running debate between those who argued that heavy industry and the defence industry were identical, and those who portrayed the two as overlapping, but essentially different.

CHAPTER FOUR

The Debate in Bloom

By late September 2002, just before a high-level US delegation finally arrived in Pyongyang, there appeared to be an uneasy stalemate within the leadership as to how the reforms would affect economic priorities, especially that afforded to the military sector. This stalemate could not last; there was bound to be a fight. It *could* have turned into a demonstration of the typical life cycle of new North Korean economic ideas—nasty, brutish and short. Instead, over the next two years, something quite different emerged.

A repetition of the old cycle would have included the recognition of problems in the economy, discussion about ways to improve performance, suggestions for a new path and, ultimately, a halt to all but the most minor changes, as orthodox arguments – that external dangers to the regime did not permit innovation – prevailed. But this time around, even a serious spike in tensions with the United States in 2003 did not bring an end to the reforms. The conservatives deployed old military first arguments in 2002 and again in 2003 in an unsuccessful effort to halt them. A new, important dynamic had emerged, in which reformers were not completely at the mercy of their opponents. This new dynamic was important because it set the stage for the subsequent rounds of the reform process.

In rough terms, two trends were developing at the same time during 2002: new attempts to define the scope and foundation of the military first ideology; and sustained efforts to move ahead with economic reforms. It is hard to imagine that these developments were not connected. The question is, were they pulling in the same direction or against each other?

The evidence suggests they represented different and, in some cases, quite opposed schools of thought.

The experience of China and Vietnam has demonstrated that economic reform does not proceed steadily, at least not in its early years. The process in North Korea will move forward and backwards and fluctuate frequently in search of temporary points of equilibrium, before reaching a relatively stable economic and political plateau.[1]

There are two points to bear in mind when considering the economic reform programme that Kim Jong Il launched in July 2002: it had been in the works for several years; and almost from the beginning there were strong indications that the particular measures announced were only intended as first (and to some extent experimental) steps. Put another way, the ideas behind the new economic policies had momentum never before possessed by such efforts. From the start, the reforms were not tentative and they were fully expected – by the reformers and most likely Kim Jong Il himself – to grow over time.

How, given emerging tensions in the international situation beginning in late 2002, were these reforms sustained? This problem is difficult for many outside observers who are distracted by the constant repetition of the term 'military first' in the North Korean media. There is a tendency to take this literally and to assume that every reference to the term constitutes a reaffirmation of it. But the military first concept is no more a sound guideline to real North Korean policy than was that of *juche* (self-reliance) in earlier years.[2] These are not policies but slogans. They capture a level of policy reality, but not all of it. References to slogans do not, in themselves, describe the totality of the issues being argued or the positions advocated. In fact, a reference to a slogan can be a commentator's sword, or his shield.

Judging by references to the military first idea in North Korean pronouncements alone, it is easy to conclude that defence spending has absolute priority. But pure repetition is a poor indicator of practice. How is this concept being put into operation and are there differences in nuance over phasing or emphasis? Is it simply a question of money or does 'first' cover priorities for resource allocation, labour and technology? How can proclamations that the defence industry comes first be justified in the North's new economic environment, and, crucially for those in charge of implementing the new policies, what are the costs to the reforms of doing so? If you are a planner or a manager, can you implement both – military first policies and reform – at the same time and if not, which do you choose? What are the costs to the reforms if you make the wrong choice? Or for that matter, what are the costs to your own livelihood and career?

North Korean officials claim that they see no contradiction between the demands of defence priorities and economic reforms. Possibly, some of them actually do not. Perhaps they hear the word 'contradiction' and imagine that it suggests a level of imperfection in centrally mandated policies that they do not wish to acknowledge. But there is another way of measuring whether or not there is a sense in Pyongyang of serious contradictions yet to be resolved between a pure interpretation of military first ideas and the emerging requirements of Kim Jong Il's instructions for new economic thinking: the steady stream of articles in the media grappling with these questions.

It is significant that the reforms themselves have barely been visible in the open North Korean media. They do not appear to have been discussed directly or explicitly. Nevertheless, a close review of media commentary from 2000 to 2005 suggests they have become a strong and, in many ways, perhaps the strongest, force transforming policies and practical economic realities within North Korea at every level. And the policy of reform has become an unseen gravitational mass in the public debate. It is against the reforms that the conservative counter-attack exploded in October 2002, and it is because of the strength of the reform process that discussions on military spending and the defence industry gradually took on a curiously apologetic tone.

None of this was clear in 2002, however. At the time, observers focused primarily on the October visit of US Assistant Secretary of State James Kelly to Pyongyang, the first such contact between a senior Bush administration official and the North Koreans. From Washington's perspective, the main focus of the visit was to be Pyongyang's nuclear weapons programme and, in the aftermath, the results have largely been seen in those terms. But the visit had an additional significance. The North Korean economic reforms were barely three months old when the American delegation arrived on 3 October. When the visit ended, two days later, it had produced something that those in Pyongyang backing the reforms did not expect and certainly did not need – a showdown with the United States over the American claim that the North was pursuing a secret programme to produce highly enriched uranium for building nuclear weapons. The confrontation may, however, have seemed like manna from heaven to those opposed to reform. A sharp deterioration in US–North Korean relations, leading towards an escalating confrontation that quickly took on military overtones, created precisely the external environment that the conservatives could profit from and that the reformers needed to avoid.

Suggesting that a confrontation with the United States was the last thing Pyongyang expected, on 5 October, the final day of the Kelly visit, *Nodong Sinmun* carried an article replete with reformist themes. It did not contain a single reference to military first ideas or the priority of defence. Instead, it emphasised that 'the scientific character of our party's economic policy is clearly expressed in that it enables one to carry out economic work in a creative manner in accordance with the *changed environment and realistic conditions'*. These conditions in which economic activities proceed 'are not fixed and unchangeable. Economic activities under a new environment are to proceed with new relationships and new rules'.[3] A new environment, new relationships, new rules for economic activities: these were three concepts likely to enrage conservatives.

Yet, on that same day, even before Kelly's aircraft had left the ground, the conservatives launched what turned out to be a sustained, forceful effort to assert the military first concept not merely as a slogan, but as a ruling ideology, dictating every aspect of national policy, organisation and priorities. A *Nodong Sinmun* editorial board special article went far beyond the three earlier articles devoted to military first in the spring and summer. It called quite literally for transforming the foundations of the North Korean regime into one which puts 'military first, workers later'.[4] Like the earlier editorial bureau articles, however, this one still did not address economic issues directly beyond noting the need for a 'strong defence industry'. It did caution that, 'it is fantasy to think that one can achieve the idea of independence without gun barrels', a challenge to anyone arguing for measures to reduce defence priorities. And it repeated earlier warnings that 'military first is not a temporary line aimed at overcoming immediate ordeals confronting us'.

There is no way to know how far in advance the article was planned, and whether it was written well before or during the Kelly visit. It is possible for something of great policy significance to be produced quickly in Pyongyang and there is a precedent for fast and authoritative North Korean reactions. In June 1973, for example, Kim Il Sung responded with a major policy address on inter-Korean relations within hours of a speech by South Korean President Park Chung Hee; the 5 October editorial bureau article could have been written overnight. It is equally likely, though, that the article had in some sense been in the minds of conservatives ever since the start of the reforms on 1 July and that they were waiting for the right moment to fire their shot. The negative course of the talks with the American delegation may have provided the target of opportunity they needed.

One observer (though referring to a later editorial board article in March 2003) has suggested that this bold assertion of military power over the party was actually a gambit by Kim Jong Il to push the Korean Workers' Party, with its decades of ideological baggage, aside, in order to create a ruling structure centred around a modernising military that could oversee the economic reform process.[5] The timing of the October editorial bureau article, however, and the subsequent struggle in the media over the next year about the meaning of military first policies in economic terms, strongly suggest that the piece was not an opening gambit to put the reforms on new, firmer ground, but rather one aimed at diverting their course, if not killing them outright.

Significantly, one of the most explicit references to the new economic policies appeared later the same month in a statement by a foreign ministry spokesman. It responded sharply to the Kelly visit and implied that Pyongyang had expected that its new economic policies would resonate more fully with American thinking. The statement noted that, 'The DPRK has taken a series of new steps in economic management and adopted one measure after another to reenergize the economy … in conformity with the changed situation and specific conditions of the country.'[6] It observed that 'these developments practically contribute to peace in Asia and the world', and that, therefore, 'almost all countries except for the United States welcomed and hailed them, a great encouragement to the DPRK'.

The remainder of 2002 was busy insofar as the nuclear question was concerned. By late autumn, after Washington's decision to force the KEDO Executive Board to halt heavy fuel-oil shipments to North Korea, Pyongyang was well on its way to ending the freeze on its nuclear activities at the Yongbyon nuclear facility, restarting its only operational reactor and preparing to withdraw from the NPT. In December, International Atomic Energy Agency inspectors were asked to leave the country and steps were underway to restart the nuclear facilities at Yongbyon.

Even as the nuclear situation continued to deteriorate, the economic reformers were asserting their position. An article in the December issue of *Kyongje Yongu*, which spelt out Kim Jong Il's principles for building a strong economy, barely paid lip-service to the demands of the military first approach.[7] It went through four principles that Kim Jong Il had advanced for building an 'economically powerful' state, noting that this was a task 'to be accomplished in an entirely different manner according to the realistic conditions we are encountering'.

The article argued that the concept of 'self-reliance' had been 'defined anew, differently from before', and that Kim had called for economic work to be performed according to the 'new concept'. It noted that 'science and technology is the basic key to the development of the country and the nation', seemingly the very position that the *Nodong Sinmun* editorial board piece in August had railed against. Finally, the article argued the need to embrace thoroughly the idea of making 'real profits in economic work'. This meant properly combining long- and short-term economic interests or, in orthodox terms, finding the right balance between accumulation and consumption. In a serious challenge to the conservatives, the article asserted that producing real economic profits meant 'properly combining political-military interests and economic interests'. The article did aver that it was necessary to put effort into strengthening defence capabilities, but claimed that it was also necessary to pay 'keen attention to providing good working conditions for the working people and *regulate production and distribution so that a reasonable portion of the national income will be appropriated for supporting the people's economic life'*.

The debate boils over

Just as the North announced its withdrawal from the NPT on 10 January 2003, the economic policy debate boiled over. The issue of the role of the defence industry became the central focus of an extended public discussion over economic priorities. As became rapidly clear, it was no longer possible for conservatives simply to assert that defence spending was supremely important. Instead, they had to advance arguments justifying the role of the defence industry in economic terms. They had to include appropriate qualifiers, accentuate the nuances, acknowledge the linkages, deal with questions of 'balance' and, eventually, even admit the need to ensure that defence priorities were 'adequately combined' with those of other economic sectors.

The markers for the debate were not that obscure. Conservative commentators insisted, where they could, on unchanging truths that must govern conduct and decisions. They objected to the reformers' references to 'new realities' which supposedly justified new approaches, though they were not above falling back on arguments about reality themselves when it was clear that 'unchanging principles' needed to be adjusted. The conservatives argued, as a matter of principle, that without a strong military, there could be no nation, no economy and no regime. They insisted that the military must come first not only in emphasis but in time. Yet, try as they might, they could not hold this position for long. Almost as soon as the literal interpretation of the military first concept met the on-coming reforms, it was forced to retreat to a new line of defence.

The new line of argument was that the defence industry was essential for a strong army which, in turn, provided the necessary environment within which the economy could develop. But the reformers countered this effectively: it could hardly be judged a sufficient rationale for developing defence industries before anything else because, to put it mildly, this process would take too long. So the conservatives were forced to resort to yet another argument – that the defence industry was not something apart from the economy, but rather was integral to it. The development of the defence industry would be good for the economy overall, it would help to develop science and technology and it would stimulate demand for resources and machines. The conservatives implicitly agreed that the defence industry might not actually produce anything valuable for economic growth, but the process of its own development would provide valuable spin-offs in the form of technological advances that the rest of the economy could use. This line of argument was strikingly similar to that deployed in the United States during the 1960s by those who believed that the huge investment in the space programme might not have an immediate economic pay-off, but that in the long run it could be counted on to spur technological development.

The conservatives also tried to base their position on the North's already existing 'unique economic structure', a highly tautological argument. Defence spending had to come first because of an economic structure that put it first. In a landscape of 'new ideas', this argument was on decidedly shaky ground, because it was this very structure that the logic of the reforms was challenging. For the reformers, the economy's structure was the problem; it would have to be revamped. Conservatives argued, for example, that the defence industry was the 'same' as heavy industry, yet there appears to have been little doubt that heavy industry could and should serve the economy more profitably than the defence sector. Questions were apparently being raised in internal discussions at the time as to how managers of heavy industry enterprises could continue to give unalloyed 'priority' to the defence industry, while responding to the new management imperatives from the centre. The defence industry could only take, not give, it could only consume, and not, in the end, produce anything of real economic value.

For their part, the reformers knew that they could not afford to question the military first concept, at least not publicly or directly, as the dominant ideological theme of the moment. But they stubbornly refused to agree that it should be allowed to dictate all economic choices. Reformist articles would routinely acknowledge military first arguments and even implicitly concur with the accepted political line of 'priority attention' for military development. Explicitly opposing it would be counter-productive.

But there were many ways to argue that 'priority' did not necessarily mean what it implied. More and more qualifiers appeared in articles dealing with economic priorities, more and more formulations of the 'yes, but' variety, that pointed to a sustained effort to break the military's stranglehold on the economy and to wrest away its ability to stymie the reforms.

Beginning in 2003, the debate broadened, as the proper place, priority, relevance, function and even economic worth of the defence industry became points at issue. The concept of 'priority' for the military came under detailed scrutiny. Reformers openly argued that Marxism, Leninism, and even Stalinism, had proved inadequate for resolving satisfactorily the question of where defence spending should fit in the overall scheme of the economy. They made it plain that they would not accept the newly enlarged version of the military first concept that emerged in the autumn of October 2002.

Opening positions

Signalling the beginning of the most intense phase in the debate over priorities, on 22 January 2003, less than two weeks after the North announced its withdrawal from the NPT, a *Nodong Sinmun* article laid out the conservative line. It asserted that giving priority to the defence industry was necessary for a strong military, which in turn would create conditions for economic development: 'The only way to check and frustrate the enemies' military and economic manoeuvres aimed at crushing us and *to create a situation favourable to economic construction* is to strengthen the barrel of the gun and further build up our revolutionary armed forces as ever victorious and invincible.'[8] In other words, 'priority' was defined not merely in terms of focus but also sequence: develop the defence industry and a strong military, then it will be possible to develop the rest of the economy.

Evidence of a response appeared quickly. On 24 January, *Nodong Sinmun* carried an article that contained, apparently for the first time in the media, Kim Jong Il's slogan calling for giving the defence industry priority, while simultaneously developing light industry and agriculture. He had apparently advanced this formulation the previous September; that four months passed before it appeared in public may in part reflect the tug of war that would have occurred behind the scenes on how to handle economic priorities in the midst of an escalating crisis with the United States. The reigning slogan, 'develop defence industry with priority', became 'develop defence industry with priority, and also develop light industry and agriculture simultaneously'. This approach was also picked up by *Minju Choson* on 5 February, which carried a poster depicting the theme of combining the defence industry with light industry and agriculture, accompanied by an article noting that only by following this line could 'the dignity of the country and the nation be defended, socialism be protected and safeguarded, and the people live affluent and civilized lives'.[9]

In late February, *Nodong Sinmun* picked up the theme that had appeared in the December 2002 *Kyongje Yongu* article. It was necessary to 'correctly resolve the correlations between the two sides: defence industry, which is directly related to these sectors, on the one hand, and light industry and agriculture, on the other hand. It is a question of how to guarantee the speed and balance of developing the two sectors that cannot be separated from one another'.[10] Adopting the time-honoured North Korean tactic used by those advocating something other than an orthodox interpretation of the current political or economic line, the article described a middle ground:

> If emphasis is placed *only* on developing light industry and agriculture because of the people's low living standards, or by contrast, importance is put *only* on the defence industry *and scant attention is paid to light industry and agriculture, a lopsided development will result in the overall construction of socialism.*[11]

It is hard to believe that even the most dedicated reformers advocated putting emphasis 'only' on light industry and agriculture, but there were certainly some in the leadership who backed a policy line that would qualify as giving 'scant attention' to light industry and agriculture. The author noted that 'it goes without saying' that the development of the defence industry 'plays a direct role in developing the overall national economy', an argument also used in several January *Nodong Sinmun* articles pushing the conservative interpretation. But he then went on to note that light industry and agriculture provided an 'important material guarantee for reinforcing defence'. In other words, those pushing for developing the defence industry first, before developing other sectors, were incorrect. To embellish his case, the author noted that it was particularly inappropriate to over-emphasise the defence industry because light industry and agriculture needed special attention, given that 'normal development of these sectors has experienced considerable setbacks due to the imperialists' maneuvers to isolate and crush our country as well as natural disasters several years in a row'.[12]

In March 2003, as the international situation deteriorated further with the invasion of Iraq and speculation about the new American doctrine of pre-emptive attack, the economic reform programme entered a new phase, which saw the establishment of general markets and authorisation of private commercial activities. Indications of the debate continued to appear in the North Korean press. A *Minju Choson* editorial on 12 March reiterated the most fundamental theme of the reformers, arguing that since the military might of North Korea had already reached a powerful state, the question now was how to carry out economic construction. It asserted that 'boosting the economy *without delay* is an important demand for strengthening national might and improving the people's living standard'.[13] The point was that if the military was important for the economy, so equally was the economy important for the military, and thus, working to improve the economy could not wait for a 'strong military' to create the 'right conditions'. Soon afterwards, *Nodong Sinmun* sounded the opposite note, asserting that a strong military was vital to 'defend sovereignty and dignity of nation'. It cheekily stole a line from the reformers about adapting policies to changing circumstances, claiming that, 'military first ... is in accord with today's realistic conditions'.[14]

The conservatives shift

As economic reforms entered a new phase in March 2003, signs appeared that the conservatives had taken a step back. Another *Nodong Sinmun* editorial bureau article appeared on 21 March, asserting that the country's future 'hinges on invincible military might', but conceding that 'a country can be regarded as a powerful state' only when it can boast of power 'not only in the political and military areas but also in the economic and cultural fields'.[15] By early April, however, the line had again toughened, reflected in a *Nodong Sinmun* editorial bureau article that waded deep into the debate: 'Once we lay the foundation for a powerful self-supporting national defence industry, we will be able to rejuvenate all economic fields, including light industry and agriculture.'[16] This was an argument not simply for priority but for sequence; real work on the parts of the economy of high interest to the reformers would have to wait for the foundations of the defence industry to be laid. Conspicuously absent from the piece (and in noticeable contrast to the 21 March editorial bureau article) was any reference to Kim Jong Il's formulation about giving priority to the defence industry while also developing light industry and agriculture.

A long piece on 9 May even suggested counter-attacks were about to become ideologically ugly and personally menacing by making a rare reference to the 1962 Cuban missile crisis, which in North Korean leadership circles serves as a reminder of 'traitors to the revolution' in the Soviet Union and Pyongyang's subsequent decisions to boost military spending in order to develop an independent defence capability.[17] 'We should not', the article warned, 'become men without faith who move according to changes in the environment and set sail according to the wind', an attack, if ever there was one, on the reformist idea of adapting to 'new conditions'. It also raised the explosive issue of money, a sensitive subject given the reforms' emphasis on material rewards and profits. 'Those who do not show firm revolutionary faith in everyday life become languid when faced with the captivating power of money and fortune as well as become weak before temptations and pain.' The piece even contained what appeared to be a veiled warning to reformers to forget about following the Chinese example: 'A cat cannot catch mice after knowing the taste of meat, and a revolutionary cannot carry out revolution after knowing the taste of money.'[18]

A few weeks later, the reply appeared in a *Minju Choson* piece, stressing that, 'The vitality of politics is indicated through actual practice. *Actual practice is the measuring standard for truth and the starting point for consciousness.* Great politics cannot but generate great realities.'[19] It would be hard to get closer to the 'Dengist' argument of discovering 'truth through practice' without actually citing Deng by name – and any North Korean reformer, or conservative, thinking about economic policy would know it. The article noted the sacrifice of the people during hard economic times of the past and their willingness to 'live without candies but not without bullets'. But it went on to argue that national military prowess was not enough, stressing that, 'even in today's difficult situation, we are relentlessly pushing ahead with our economic construction'.[20]

Reformers also raised the issue of the development of markets, a subject not normally addressed in the media. A 10 June KCNA commentary, while ostensibly complaining that the United States was maligning the North over drug-trafficking and terrorism, also noted that the North had recently passed new laws on markets. Pyongyang hoped 'to receive as much cooperation as possible from other countries including expert training and experience as it is the first time for it to run such markets'.[21] This was a plea straight from the heart of the reformers, who made similar requests to audiences overseas, noting that reform would need to show 'results' fairly soon or face severe questioning from its critics.

A few days later, a *Nodong Sinmun* editorial signalled the beginning of a new phase in the debate, in which the conservatives struck a decidedly defensive note over the central question of the real cost of military spending versus that of economic development. The editorial claimed that the army was 'managing its economy meticulously on its own lest burdens should be imposed on the state and the people'.[22] What was needed in assisting the armed forces was not 'material assistance' but rather 'ideological and spiritual assistance … rendered consistent with the nature, mission, and superiority of the KPA [Korean People's Army]'. The piece did not directly address how, in the military first era, the armed forces – supposedly the central pillar of the revolution and the priority for economic activity – did not 'impose [economic] burdens' on the state and the people.

The defensive tone continued over the following days. Another *Nodong Sinmun* article squarely picked up the issue of what contribution defence spending made to overall economic development. Brushing aside the idea that there was a contradiction between building military and economic power since 'the issue of building strong national economic power is also linked to the issue of strengthening military power', it then launched into a curious rationale for continued defence spending not only on military, but also economic grounds.[23] The article asserted that it was short-sighted to believe that the 'army is a pure consumer and expenditures for national defence are merely non-productive expenditures'. Rather, 'defence industry, heavy industry, and light industry, which are the major sectors of the economy, *are closely linked to each other*'. In effect, spending on the defence industry would stimulate the rest of the economy, because its preferential development 'will bring about development of science and technology and at the same time give a stir to development of heavy industry related to defence industry'.[24]

Whereas the reformers had argued that attention to light industry and agriculture was important because these sectors support the defence sector, this article turned that logic upset down, contending:

> Defence industry is related not only to heavy industry but also to all domains of national economy, including light industry. In fact, today's defence industry is considered so important an industrial sector as to represent the level of the nation's economic development and economic power. Indeed, defence industry is a lifeline in building a powerful and wealthy fatherland, and *concentrating efforts on strengthening military power is to serve as an important guarantee for strengthening the nation's economic power*.[25]

These efforts to justify defence spending on economic grounds suggest that the reformers were gaining ground and that the once-sacred military cow was finding itself increasingly harried. The notion that the defence sector was 'non-productive' surfaced again in the August 2003 volume of *Kyongje Yongu*, in an article ostensibly criticising capitalist practice, but which could equally be read as being aimed closer to home. In the capitalist economic process the 'militarization of economy increases *non-productive consumption*, which hampers preferential growth of accumulation ... and expands and intensifies the contradictions between accumulation and production. This causes a general expansion of the munitions production sector and related sectors, thereby intensifying imbalance among economic sectors'.[26]

In September 2003, the conservatives brandished a 15-year-old Kim Il Sung speech to bolster their case. A *Nodong Sinmun* article on 8 September argued, 'Military matters are *among the most important* state affairs and all industries should be subordinated to strengthening the national defence capability.'[27] And a few days later another article in the same newspaper tried knocking the reformers again by reviving the old canard about the dangers of completely ignoring the military: 'Neglecting the work of strengthening the national defence capability for the sake of the country's economic prosperity and improving the people's material life is as good as flinging open the doors of the country to the imperialists.'[28]

But these attacks turned out to be dying embers rather than a new blaze of conservative opposition. By contrast, the reformers seemed to have become invigorated. A *Nodong Sinmun* article on 25 November began with a quotation from Kim Jong Il that put the economy and national defence on an equal plane: 'By unremittingly waging a vigorous struggle for strengthening the might of a self-reliant national economy and self-defensive national defence capability, we have to further reinforce the material foundation of an independent state and social life and reliably safeguard the safety of the country and happy lives of the people.'[29] The article, stressing the importance of information technology in formulating and executing more scientific and modern military operations, asserted that 'such a characteristic of modern warfare raises a pressing need to guarantee the production of modern military equipment by modernizing and informatizing all sectors of the national economy'.[30] And after the usual bow to the role of heavy industry in supporting the defence industry, the article went on, 'The modernization and informatization of light industry and agriculture are also important factors that enable the construction of a powerful defence industry.' Those sectors, in other words, could not be left behind or told to wait.

By December 2003, signs that the tide had shifted appeared. Using a tactic often employed by North Korean factions engaged in an uphill fight, conservatives tried to demonstrate that their position enjoyed international support in the form of a Pyongyang radio report on a Pakistani newspaper article repeating the standard line that spending on defence was good for the economy.[31] Later that same month, a *Nodong Sinmun* editorial bureau special article sounded a note of retreat. Launching a stiff attack on any attempt at 'doing away with ideology', 'depoliticization' of the army, 'separating party and army from one another' or 'separating politics and army from one another', it branded all these as 'reactionary sophistry that repudiates the class character of the gun barrel and blunts the will of the gun barrel'.[32] The argument suggested a high degree of sensitivity on the part of the conservatives, as well as an effort to rally against arguments that were either already in circulation or that they feared were soon to wash over them.

Implicitly, this effort to emphasise the overwhelming need to arm the military with a strong ideology accepted the notion that a materially well-equipped military is not the key to success. That notion seemed to lead naturally to further discussion that represented a major retreat from previous conservative arguments. The author admitted that 'the work of defence build-up, economic construction and improving the people's standard of living' should be achieved 'by meshing them closely with one another'. After admitting that the standard of living should be 'decisively improved' by 'simultaneously developing light industry and agriculture while putting prime effort into developing our defence industry', the article surprisingly asserted that 'by tightly grasping our party's seed theory, [functionaries] should become friendly comrades who will do everything innovatively and in a way of *producing actual profits*'.

Conservatives, unlike reformers, did not normally talk about 'closely meshing' defence build-up, economic construction and the standard of living. They did not, if they could help it, talk about 'profits'. If they had to discuss profits, they looked for ways to undercut or dilute the concept. Yet here was an editorial board article embracing both. Since it is unlikely that the reformers had taken over the editorial room at *Nodong Sinmun*, one might conclude that at this point, the conservatives, however uncomfortable it may have been for them, had been forced to make significant concessions to the reformers.

The conservatives seem to have been down but not out. In another *Nodong Sinmun* article in late January 2004, they tried to regain their footing, framing the economic issue again in terms of sequenced development, but this time granting the existence of an important linkage between military power and overall economic progress. The article asserted that 'no matter how abundant a country's natural resources and how wealthy its material economy, it cannot be called a strong nation if its military power is weak'.[33] The logic was that a strong economy and weak military led to overall weakness. The article also revived the argument that defence spending was an economic stimulus by providing the 'newest science and technology of this sector to various sectors of the people's economy'.[34]

Even Pyongyang's 10 February 2005 announcement that it had become a nuclear-weapons state contained what appeared to be a nasty dig at the reforms: 'If the United States really wants to have talks, it can just have talks with peasant market merchants, whom the United States is said to like.'[35] Peasant merchants may have been doing too brisk a business to have noticed, but a shiver might well have run up the spine of those in the leadership who were committed to pushing the new economic policies.

Reformers push the limits

By coincidence, a number of articles appeared in the year's first quarterly issue of *Kyongje Yongu* that same day, advancing more forcefully than ever the reformist answer to the question of military priorities. These articles flatly contradicted any notions about putting economic construction in second place. One of the pieces approached the problem not from the stand-point of theory, but of practice, observing that since 'the military first era consists of a national defence industry and civilian industry, we also divide planning indicators into military production indicators and civilian produc-tion indicators in carrying out economic work'.[36] Given the military first principle, 'we must place importance on military production indicators before anything else'. That meant the 'priority provision of labour' for devel-oping the national defence industry and, in particular, 'priority provision of workers with high scientific and technical knowledge and skills in line with the demand for modernizing the national defence industry'.

But then the article switched gear, emphasising that much more than the defence sector had to be considered: 'Machinery, basic resources, mate-rials, electricity and other things must be provided so that production may proceed. *The important mission before the materials supply sector is to supply these means of production in all areas of the people's economy.'* And that meant providing for production as a priority for the military logistics sector while guaranteeing overall economic construction as well. On the all-important question of funds, the article made clear that 'we confer priority signifi-cance in national budget expenditures to budget outlays for strengthening the country's defence capability *while at the same time guaranteeing the neces-sary budget expenditure for general economic construction and improving people's lives.'* To accomplish these seemingly impossible tasks, it noted, a cabinet-centred government had been established (i.e., one of the measures of the 1998 constitution) with the cabinet appointed as 'an economic headquar-ters'. This surely caused a stir; the cabinet had not only been given extra responsibilities for running the economy but had also been put in charge of developing and implementing the reforms.

A second article in the same *Kyongje Yongu* issue picked up where the first had left off. Agreeing that the development of the defence industry was 'the primary strategic task in revolution and construction', it added that the military first line also *'combines defence build-up and economic construction with the issue of people's living standards in the most correct manner, so that all of them can be successfully resolved at the highest possible level'*.[37] This formulation was identical to the 22 December 2003 *Nodong Sinmun* editorial bureau article, reinforcing the impression that it was a reformist line the conservatives had no choice but to accept.

The *Kyongje Yongu* piece, however, went beyond the idea of 'combining' work on defence-building and economic construction, implying that work on the economy must precede the defence build-up. Also combining the threads of the reformist argument on how economic development and military development reinforced each other, it asserted that economic construction involved 'not only the tasks and *methods to strengthen defence industry but also those to further consolidate the country's defence capabilities and dramatically enhance the people's living standards by powerfully stepping up overall economic development'*.[38] Economic development and the 'dramatic' enhancement of living standards, in other words, could not be an eventual outcome but had to be a near-term, tangible result in order to motivate the people. Giving the people the prospect of economic improvement was as important a task as strengthening defence industries.

If the February 2004 *Kyongje Yongu* contained the anvil for the reformists, then the May issue contained the hammer, an innocent-sounding article entitled 'Several Theoretical Issues for the Military First Era's Reproduction'.[39] In substance anything but innocent, this piece dissected the basis of the military's favoured position in the national economy, examining the economic worth of the defence industry and coming to the shattering conclusion that this sector is essentially 'non-productive'. The article broached this difficult and dangerous subject by asserting that if the conservatives wished to talk about the military first concept as a new organising principle, then they must look beyond a literal interpretation of the words and examine all of its manifestations and ramifications closely.

The essence of the argument was that, in the military first era in which 'the significance and role of war supplies have become larger', it is crucial to determine where war supplies fit in the overall economic scheme. This is not an argument that directly confronts the question of the defence industry per se, but rather puts the production of the defence industry (i.e., war supplies) under the microscope. According to the article, war supplies fit neither the classical definition of 'accumulation' nor that of 'consumption'. They do not support expanded production, nor do they enhance the people's lives or meet their short-term needs. They are somewhat similar to consumer goods, however, in terms of being used '*to satisfy non-productive consuming needs*'.

While the author carefully covers himself by praising the role of war supplies in strengthening the country's defence capabilities and becoming 'immediate constituents in the wealth of the people' even when in storage, he asserts that war supplies:

> must be considered as an individual form of social production along with the means of production and consumption materials. *Under the condition where the actual forms of the products of society are divided not into two but three, it would be more judicious to also divide social production into three sectors: the sector producing war supplies, the sector producing means of production, and the sector producing consumption materials.*

The national defence industry, in other words, cannot share the table with accumulation and consumption, heavy industry and light industry. It must find its own table and, if it sits at its own table, it cannot eat from the same bowl as the others.

Spelling out the implications of separating heavy industry from the defence industry, a task that earlier reformist authors had taken up but never finished, the article asserts that 'a balance must be established' between the three categories of social production. But such a balance is complicated given that goods produced in the defence sector 'cannot be put into the reproduction process, and in forming a reproduction relationship with other production sectors, the defence sector can only receive but not give produced goods'. Production from the national defence industry is therefore of limited value to the economy overall. In a word, it is parasitic. The author even rejects the old conservative argument that the defence industry is an incubator for scientific and technological development that feeds into the economy, observing that the sector does not share its real assets but tends to monopolise talent, which ends up serving only a non-productive segment of the economy.

The article's real hammer blows are directed at the central question of the allocation of resources. Again, the author suggests that the issue comes down to definitions, and specifically, definitions of accumulation and consumption. After defining accumulation as 'a form of utilizing national income for the people's future happiness, and consumption as a form of utilizing national income to satisfy immediate demands', the article notes that, essentially, accumulation should contribute to expanding production. But, *'things that contribute to strengthening national defence capabilities cannot be included in the content of accumulation'* because military 'equipment for the purpose of dealing with the enemies' invasive schemes is not charged with the mission of enhancing the people's future lives'. Nor can military equipment, 'prepared through the preferential growth of the national defence industry be consumed in kind because it is not used in the people's present lives, either'. That means the production from the national defence industry promises no material advantage for the people.

Yet such production must surely amount to something. Since it is not consumption – a sector of national income for satisfying the people's immediate needs – it must fall into the category of accumulation. 'The scale of accumulation of war supplies and the reciprocal relations between accumulation and consumption must be newly established under the condition where war supplies are not a form of consumption but a form of accumulation.' Establishing the proper place for war supplies in the economic scheme is not a teleological exercise. There is actually a vital principle at stake: the ratio between accumulation and consumption. 'Preferentially enhancing accumulation while simultaneously making consumption grow is a principle that we have strictly adhered to in establishing a balance between accumulation and consumption … *Based on this principle in the past, our party converted approximately one fourth of the national income to accumulation and approximately three fourths to consumption.'*

Put another way, if war supplies are counted as consumption, and their role is increasing, then that leaves *less* for real consumption. But if war supplies are counted as accumulation – along with other spending (e.g., heavy industry) that is allocated to the military – then that will at least not reduce and may actually help lessen the reduction of resources for other, 'productive' areas of the economy.

The boldness of the argument – that the national defence industry is non-productive and that a new way must be devised to figure the real costs of defence spending – is itself a sign of how far the reformers have come and, at the same time, an indication of how far they have to go.

CHAPTER FIVE

Implications and Conclusions

It will almost certainly not be clear for some years whether North Korea's most profound economic reform programme, begun in 2002, will succeed. Overall, while growth in the North Korean economy has been positive since 1999 and predates the reform package, this has occurred largely because of assistance from China, South Korea and other foreign sources. The annual growth rate of 2% falls far short of other so-called 'economies in transition' like Vietnam, where GDP increased by an average of 4% a year from 1986 to 1990 and by more than 8% annually from 1990 to 1997. China has achieved an average annual growth of more than 8% since 1978 in spite of potential drags such as a much larger population and a less-educated workforce.[1]

In the short run, it is important to bear in mind that ideas do not simply travel downwards from the top in Pyongyang. It is true that initiatives on politically sensitive topics may be impeded, but new economic ideas are apparently no longer considered quite so sensitive. No doubt there are still boundaries to economic discussions, but these boundaries have been expanded since 2002, and there are not yet signs of any new contraction. For the next few years, it will be important for outside observers not to over-react to daily developments. The question should not be whether specific measures have been reversed, but rather whether the subject of economic reform is still open to discussion within the leadership.

In early 2006, the process of reform was apparently continuing. The premier still appears frequently with Kim Jong Il – a sign that not only the individual but also the ideas he represents remain in good standing. In January 2006, Kim Jong Il again visited areas of southern China that are associated with the early days, and fruits, of Chinese economic reform. There are other signs of the emergence of new ideas, though the details may not always be clear.[2]

The political impetus may continue but there is no guarantee that reform will succeed. There remain five significant obstacles to it. Firstly, the ruling elite today must confront the same challenge it has faced since the 1960s when the North Korean leadership first realised the shortcomings of communism. How does it reconcile the need for reform with the threat that change poses for the regime's very survival? This is the dilemma faced by Kim Jong Il, who obviously has the most at stake, as well as the bureaucracy and the military. That dilemma is reflected in the active debate among the elite.

Secondly, North Korea's government faces a major fiscal challenge – a cash-flow crisis – that constrains the ability of reformers to address critical problems. Because of this crisis, budget constraints imposed by Pyongyang on enterprises have resulted in at least 30% of the working age population being under-employed or unemployed, increasing the likelihood of social instability. North Korea is also stuck in the classic 'poverty trap', in that it does not possess sufficient production capacity to satisfy domestic demand or to compensate for capital depreciation. This is caused by a steady 'industrial degeneration' that affects key sectors such as energy production and the transport network.

Thirdly, even a sustained North Korean commitment to reform would have little or no chance of succeeding without the right external environment and access to international assistance and financing. The steady deterioration in relations with the United States and Japan – the two countries most important in helping to gain access to this assistance – that began in 2002 with the disclosure of suspicions about Pyongyang's secret uranium-enrichment programme and Kim Jong Il's confession that North Korea had abducted Japanese citizens, has led both countries to oppose any such assistance.

Fourthly, North Korea is not prepared to adapt to a market economy. Unlike many other transitional economies which have had previously positive experiences with capitalism, Pyongyang's colonial experience with Japan and its 60 years of Stalinist command economics and communist orthodoxy have left it with no such historical memories. If anything, that historical experience may serve to reinforce a yearning for the 'good old days'. This state of affairs, combined with the lack of knowledge in the bureaucracy of market economics, the absence of a business environment conducive to foreign investment, and poor management techniques and systems that obstruct growth has created a significant 'knowledge divide'.

Fifthly, crony capitalism appears to be widespread, with corruption infecting virtually every sector of the economy. For example, according to one expert, the estimated 150,000 state security service operatives use their status, knowledge and access to benefit from illegal activities such as smuggling, customs evasion and assistance to individuals seeking to enter China illicitly. Extortion and kickbacks pervade business dealings with North Korean officials.[3]

While all of this would not seem to bode well for the future of economic reform, and the short-term results may appear disappointing when compared with other transitional economies, it is worth noting that the politics of economic reform in North Korea may turn out to be similar to the experience of other countries. According to one study of China, 'the process of economic policy making ... has been considerably less incremental than the results of reform would seem to indicate'.[4] Since the goals and methods of reform have been the subject of sharp debate throughout the process, 'economic policy has had a lurching, discontinuous quality that contrasts with the generally more incremental process of marketization'.[5] Indeed, China's leaders also faced difficult choices in the course of reform and were bound to encounter problems whichever course they chose. At this point, no one can say how Pyongyang will handle these challenges, but the description of the process would also seem to apply to North Korea.

Recent developments in the country's economic reform programme may reflect this lurching quality. In late 2005, press reports indicated that Pyongyang had taken steps to revitalise its public distribution system for food – which had collapsed in the mid-1990s – along with other measures, such as a revival of food rationing and a ban on trade in grain. These moves were interpreted by experts as turning back the clock on reforms and strengthening state control of the economy.[6] Another interpretation, based on first-hand contact with North Koreans, is that they saw this move as a way to combat inflation by bringing down the price of rice.[7] Nevertheless, the implementation of the measure was certainly imperfect, for example, the rice was available only for workers in state enterprises and not the urban unemployed, and probably also reflected a political motive as well. In short, these measures may have represented a step back on the path towards reform but the reasons are not nearly as clear cut as some experts would assert. Indeed, they may have been taken, in part, to allow reforms to continue.

Moreover, when these steps are placed in the context of other discussions taking place, the picture emerging is of an economic reform process that is alive and well. In late 2005, an important meeting held in Pyongyang on the occasion of the fortieth anniversary of a Kim Il Sung work on 'Unified and Detailed Planning' evidently discussed much more than centralised economic guidance, also touching on marketisation. In a press interview on 19 October, an official from the DPRK Central Planning Commission observed that the situation today is much different than when the 'classic work' by Kim Il Sung was published, namely that the cooperating economies of the socialist bloc no longer exist. As a result, state-owned enterprises must be supplemented by other markets for exchanging materials and resources with capitalist countries and for distributing consumer goods to the people.[8] A subsequent article in *Kyongje Yongu* called for 'correctly combining the socialist planned economy with commercial activities'.[9]

One factor that has been missing from most analysis of the current situation in North Korea has been recognition of the strong, and surprising, political impetus behind reform. This is particularly true of what appears to be the emerging and growing debate over whether the high levels of resource commitment to national defence can continue if reforms are to move forward. Focusing on North Korean pronouncements about military first politics without reading the fine print, which reflects a very active and growing internal debate on this subject, has impeded recognition of this debate let alone any effort to understand and analyse its implications for North Korea's future.

What is perhaps even more surprising is that the debate in North Korea has raged, and even strengthened, in spite of the deteriorating external security environment which in the past would have been sufficient to stifle reform. Conservatives have tried to use all the arguments at their disposal to derail the reform process but, even in the context of what from their perspective constitutes a favourable external security situation, have failed. The most recent manifestation of the internal debate, the articles appearing in the February and May 2004 issues of *Kyongje Yongyu*,[10] signal the beginning of a potentially startling phase of the internal discussion, in which the argument is made that the defence sector of the economy has been non-productive and this fact of life should no longer be swept under the economic rug. Whether this assertion, which would have constituted heresy in the past, continues to be reflected in the North Korean media will be an important indicator of the direction of the debate.

The key question is whether this strong impetus can be maintained. While it would be easier at least to start answering this question if we could clearly identify all the players in this debate as it unfolds, that task is presently almost impossible. But the views of the most important participant

– Kim Jong Il – are less obscure. Many would argue, justifiably, that he has the most to lose if the current system collapses. According to one recent study, 'his hereditary succession also makes the repudiation of past policies much more problematic so he lacks the revisionist power of authoritarian reformers like China's Deng Xiaoping or South Korea's Park Chung Hee'.[11] But in fact, Kim Jong Il may be ideally suited to push economic reform forward since he is Kim Il Sung's son and, therefore, cannot be accused of revisionism or of betraying his father's legacy.

In fact, Kim Jong Il seems to have a long history of supporting 'change' in the North Korean system that dates back at least to the early 1970s and his support of the 'three revolution teams'. Granted, this initiative, which involved sending young people to factories to encourage greater productivity, smacked more of Chairman Mao Zedong's Cultural Revolution than of Western capitalism. But his support demonstrated Kim Jong Il's long awareness of the dead hand of the Korean Workers' Party on economic issues and was the beginning of his unending search for pragmatic, effective steps that might bolster the economy. Beginning in the early 1990s, he nurtured leadership elements who were touting economic reforms and is reported to have written an article criticising the existing 'administrative control system' as a vestige of the past.[12] And, as already noted, he seems to have lent his support to change, for example, through signalling his approval of 'profits' as a guiding theme in new economic plans in 2001, as well as his trips to China to demonstrate his personal interest and to show sceptics the positive results of reform.

As past experience of economic transition elsewhere has demonstrated, strong leadership is absolutely necessary to foster reform. That was certainly true in China. Deng, a supporter of marketisation and economic diversification, opening to the outside world and higher rates of growth, initially worked closely with other party leaders, but broke with them in 1984 at the Third Plenary Session of the Twelfth Central Committee which inaugurated a new 'second wave' of reform, with measures going well beyond those previously taken. Deng, however, did not silence conservatives. He pursued a 'divide and rule' strategy which had a number of advantages including helping him to maintain his central position of influence. Kim Jong Il certainly occupies a much stronger position than Deng ever did. But his personal style, while perhaps more autocratic than his father's, has also been to permit discussion within certain parameters. This accounts for the muffled, on-going debate. If this analysis of his views is correct, he does support reform and that will certainly be an important factor in determining the future course of events.

Even for Kim Jong Il, this support cannot be separated from serious questions of political power, the chief one being the succession. On his sixtieth birthday Kim Il Sung essentially anointed his son as his designated successor and started a process of transition that lasted over two decades until his death in 1994. Now 63 years old, Kim Jong Il has yet to take steps to name one of his three sons as his successor. It remains unclear exactly why he has not done so. Some speculate that none of them fit the bill. For example, his eldest son Kim Jong Nam, who was apprehended trying to enter Japan to visit Tokyo's Disneyland, has not been home for years. According to press reports, the second son, Kim Jong Un, does not seem to be in favour with his father while the youngest son remains a mystery.[13] As an alternative, some Chinese experts speculate that, rather than name a successor, Kim Jong Il intends to designate a collegial body to govern North Korea during a transitional period and then to hand over power at the appropriate moment to one of his sons.[14]

It is possible that Kim Jong Il could delay addressing the problem of succession, allowing reforms to take root and avoiding potential difficulties. However, if separating the two proves impossible, he will face two difficult problems. Firstly, the exact nature of the transition will have important implications for the future of reform. Going the 'collegial route' would almost certainly make reform more difficult, perhaps dooming the process. On the other hand, if he is followed by an ineffectual successor as the result of an abbreviated or unsuccessful transition, that would also not augur well for pushing the economic reforms North Korea so desperately needs through. Thus, he will need to be careful to secure a succession sufficiently resilient to continue moving forward with the reform process.

A second, closely related issue is the difficult choice Kim Jong Il faces between a 'tactical' or 'strategic' approach. If he decides to move forward with anointing one of his sons, he will certainly need to secure support from key groups inside the North Korean elite for his designated successor, particularly important segments of the military leadership. These groups may be one and the same as, or at least overlap with, conservatives in the debate over economic reform and particularly those who seek to protect the defence establishment. He may, therefore, have to moderate his views on reform in order to secure their support or, thinking strategically, seek to maintain the momentum behind reform while gathering support for his preferred candidate by co-opting or eliminating any potential opposition. In short, aside from the challenging economic decisions that are likely to confront North Korean leaders, maintaining political momentum may also involve some difficult trade-offs.

Predicting the future of reform is difficult. Even under the most favourable circumstances, there is no guarantee that reform will be successful. How the process plays out, however, also may have an important broader effect on the future of North Korean security and foreign policy. Three scenarios seem plausible:

Growing recognition in Pyongyang that the North will need a more favourable external security environment if reforms are to be sustained

In 2002 North Korea decided to move forward with reforms in spite of the unfavourable external security environment. In this scenario, reforms may progress, but Pyongyang may come to understand that continuation will be difficult, if not impossible, as long as the external environment remains hostile. As a result, conservative opponents would be pushed aside. In addition, the North could become increasingly uncomfortable with its growing dependence on China for political and economic support and could decide to renew efforts to secure a suitable counterweight. This would lead to Pyongyang re-invigorating its engagement with the United States, Japan and maybe others such as the European Union. Better relations would, in turn, feed the further development of economic reform by providing greater access to international financial and economic assistance, bilateral assistance from others – particularly South Korea – and greater opportunities for North Koreans to develop the necessary managerial and technical skills to make their transition successful.

Such a course of action could have a number of practical consequences. First and foremost, North Korea could prove more flexible in the Beijing Six Party Talks in addressing the concerns of the United States and others about its nuclear weapons programme. Flexibility probably would not mean that Pyongyang would compromise on its basic positions, which would include a settlement that would: fully involve the United States from the very beginning (rather than allowing Washington to hang back along the lines of the 'Libya model'); include concrete steps towards satisfying the North's security concerns such as a credible security guarantee; meet Pyongyang's desire for political and economic normalisation with Washington; and satisfy its requirement for tangible assistance such as addressing energy bottlenecks in its economy.

Pyongyang might, however, be willing to play a number of cards intended to propel the negotiations forward. One example could be deferring the resolution of the issue of the North eventually securing light-water reactors, leaving it for a later day, as long as its rights in this regard are clearly acknowledged. Instead, Pyongyang might focus on the near-term provision of conventional energy sources. Moreover, in the context of striking a mutually acceptable deal, the North might even prove more cooperative than anticipated in implementing its terms for de-nuclearisation. Past experience has shown – in the early stages of implementing the 1994 US –North Korea Agreed Framework – that Pyongyang can be highly cooperative and move quickly in resolving important technical issues in the right political circumstances.

Aside from the Six Party Talks, Pyongyang could also seek progress on other fronts. A number of negotiations are likely to be jump-started by any significant progress or diplomatic solution in Beijing. For example, discussions to normalise relations with Japan could gain new momentum. While those talks would focus on eliminating the threat posed by North Korea's ballistic missile programme and addressing the issue of Japanese citizens abducted by North Korea, the pay-off for Pyongyang would be economic, in the form of significant assistance from Tokyo. The North might cooperate with efforts by South Korea and others to replace the existing state of hostilities on the Korean peninsula with permanent peace arrangements and even participate in negotiations to reduce conventional forces on both sides of the de-militarised zone. If successful, these efforts could transform the security environment on the peninsula, creating the right atmosphere for Pyongyang to reduce its large conventional forces and to shrink its huge military economic burden.

A continued struggle over reform and an inability to act decisively on key security–foreign policy issues

In this scenario, the North Korean leadership may not be able to overcome the most difficult barriers to fundamental economic reform. The process stalls because of economic problems encountered or for other reasons, for example: a loss of political momentum as the current leadership retreats from its push for reform; Kim Jong Il seeks to gather support from conservatives for a successful transition of power to one of his sons; or the ground is prepared for putting a collegial body in place. The result is a partially reformed system that breeds increasing dissatisfaction at all levels of society, leading to internal tensions and maybe even a leadership characterised by shrill, brittle, inflexible ideology.

The struggle between pro-reform and anti-reform elements could spill over into foreign policy, with anti-reform elements seeking to take advantage of (or even to create) increased tensions in order to make their case that the external environment makes reforms not only dangerous, but suicidal. Indeed, the longer the reform programme lasts and the wider it spreads, the more likely it is that the contradictions in the leadership will sharpen. Any moves towards re-engagement with other countries could be thwarted by sharp divisions inside the North Korean elite. Pyongyang's foreign policy could indeed become unpredictable and maybe even prone to taking greater risks. Moreover, North Korea's nuclear-weapons programme could become a key bone of contention inside the leadership between conservatives who see it as absolutely essential to the regime's continued survival and others who see it merely as a bargaining chip with the outside world. As a result, it may be much harder for Pyongyang to move decisively or to agree any deals in Beijing that smack of de-nuclearisation. Likewise, it could be paralysed on all other diplomatic fronts, unable to reach out to Japan or others, such as the European Union.

Progress in reform strengthens conservatives, leading to hopes in Pyongyang that it can improve the economy, while simultaneously maintaining a large, powerful military

In this scenario, reform may move forward and signs might appear – such as new growth – that the economy is improving over an extended period of time. The process would be fuelled by continued economic assistance from China and South Korea, with other countries essentially watching from the sidelines. While supporters of reform may argue for the need to continue to move forward, slow improvement might strengthen the position of their conservative opponents. They might be in a better position to argue that further advancing reform, particularly addressing the serious problems posed by the disproportionate amount of national resources devoted to the military, is no longer necessary. And that position could resonate widely in the elite since, when given the option, most North Korean leaders – perhaps even Kim Jong Il himself – would like to possess both a large powerful military and a more productive economy.

This posture would require North Korea to perform a delicate foreign and security policy balancing act. Pyongyang would continue to participate in any and all diplomatic discussions that hold out hope of peacefully resolving differences with other countries over nuclear weapons and other issues. North Korea's real intentions would remain murky but, given new optimism that it could maintain a powerful military and a more productive economy, it would be extremely difficult, if not impossible, to find acceptable compromises that would convince the North to relinquish these programmes. In this context, the North would also seek to maintain close relations with China in order to forestall any movement towards taking tougher measures against it should negotiations prove unproductive, and to secure continued economic support for its reform measures. At the same time, the North would also keep trying to build better relations with South Korea so as, at the very least, to maintain the current level of economic and other assistance it receives from Seoul. Achieving this objective might prove challenging if Washington became more frustrated with what it believed were the North's stalling tactics.

Whichever scenario plays out will have important implications for the future of the Korean peninsula, Northeast Asia and US national security policy. Washington's policy towards North Korea over the past 15 years has focused on ending North Korea's nuclear programme, as well as emphasising broader American concern about Pyongyang's ballistic missiles and its chemical- and biological-weapons programmes. That concern has certainly been justified given the dangers these programmes pose to American allies, US forces in the region and the international non-proliferation regime. But there is a broader, longer-term American foreign-policy objective which remains central to the task of building peace and stability in the region. That objective is the de-militarisation of the Korean peninsula and particularly of North Korea which, as a proportion of its population, has the largest armed forces in Asia. Such a process would entail, in addition to dealing with Pyongyang's weapons of mass destruction and missile programmes, significant reductions in its conventional forces. Presumably, part of that process would also involve building more normal, peaceful relations between the North and its neighbours.

While those analysts of North Korea who view the military first idea as a one-dimensional policy have difficulty imagining a de-militarised future, that future may indeed be possible. Certainly, North Korean policy-makers have had the opportunity to observe and study two important examples of such a process in Russia and China. It is quite likely that Kim Jong Il and others in the reform camp have been watching the process of military cutbacks in Russia closely, where President Vladimir Putin, whom Kim Jong Il has met many times, has been struggling with the same problem. Putin's public pronouncements that Russia deserves to have a military it can afford resonate with the reform camp in Pyongyang. While there have been no clear public manifestations of this interest, echoes can be found in articles by advocates of reform, particularly pronouncements that resources devoted to the military do not contribute to overall economic development. North Korea must also be aware of the two-decades-long effort by China's leaders to scale back its huge military in order to free up additional resources for economic growth. Moreover, one theme of this reform effort since it began in

1978, which also might resonate in certain circles in Pyongyang, is the need to convert China's vast military industrial complex to civilian production.

There have already been signs that the North Koreans are thinking about how to cut their massive military while maintaining a strong defence capacity. For example, Pyongyang has announced that, in response to the American nuclear threat, it will have no choice but to build up its own nuclear-deterrent force. But an authoritative pronouncement also asserted on one occasion that:

- the DPRK's intention to build up a nuclear deterrent force is not aimed to threaten and blackmail others but reduce conventional weapons under a long-term plan and channel manpower resources and funds into economic construction and the betterment of people's living.
- the DPRK will build up a powerful physical deterrent force capable of neutralizing any sophisticated and nuclear weapon with less spending unless the US gives up its hostile policy toward the DPRK.[15]

The idea that building a nuclear deterrent would enable a country to cut its conventional forces is, of course, not new to Americans who experienced a similar debate under the Eisenhower administration during the 1950s. While this approach would surely not meet with approval in Washington or elsewhere, it is a clear sign that some elements in the North Korean leadership, probably associated with economic reform, have begun to grapple with the difficult question of reducing conventional forces while maintaining an adequate defence posture.

Whether Washington can do anything at this point to influence directly the emerging debate in Pyongyang is unclear but it can certainly help to create the right context to enhance the chances for success of North Korean advocates of reform. An important first step would be to recognise that a debate over 'guns versus butter' is unfolding, to look beyond the military first sloganeering and to read the fine print. Part of that process may require devoting the necessary intelligence and other resources to develop more information on the debate, and keeping tabs on the discussion as it moves forward. This will be difficult given the closed nature of North Korean society, but even reading the official media closely can yield important clues. Part of the process may also entail making sure key US decision-makers are aware of this debate. That will require solving a much larger problem, a general lack of understanding about what is going on in North Korea, in spite of the explosion of information about the country over the past decade, which resulted from the Clinton administration's policy of engaging Pyongyang and the resultant cooperative programmes between the North and other governments, international organisations and non-governmental organisations.

But the United States also needs to consider whether it can implement a policy initiative on the Korean peninsula that would both serve American interests directly and create the right context for reform in North Korea to move forward. Re-engaging North Korea on a broad political and economic front might synergise with the reform debate to produce surprising, positive results, while boosting efforts to secure peace and stability on the peninsula and in East Asia more broadly. There might be other benefits as well. Such an initiative could help to reinvigorate US–South Korean relations. While the bilateral alliance has suffered because of domestic changes in the South – in particular the coming of political age of a new generation that is more sceptical of the value of close relations with the United States – an important contributing factor has been the current US administration's more hostile view of engagement than that of the South. A positive engagement initiative would be warmly welcomed by China which has been quietly frustrated by the Bush administration's cautious posture towards the North. Such an initiative would help to prevent potentially widening fissures between Washington and Tokyo, which now seems increasingly interested in pursuing its own bilateral engagement with North Korea in spite of American policy. These emerging differences are reflected in Japan's separate bilateral dialogue with Pyongyang, fitful though it may be.

At the core of a new American initiative would be the imperative to work bilaterally and multilaterally to de-militarise the Korean peninsula. That would mean, first and foremost, a sustained and serious bilateral effort, in the context of the Beijing Six Party Talks, to negotiate a solution to the nuclear crisis. The Bush administration's approach in Beijing has so far fallen far short of such an effort. There has been some improvement following the president's re-election in November 2004, but the United States still seems to be essentially paralysed by bureaucratic differences between 'engagers' and 'ideologues' who view any serious negotiation with Pyongyang as morally distasteful. This camp would prefer to wait until the North somehow disappears from the international scene. The overall result of this paralysis has been to allow North Korea to divide and conquer, since other participants in the Six Party Talks are not entirely sure whether American or North Korean policy is to blame for the current stalemate. And that, in turn, has allowed Pyongyang to build up its small nuclear weapons stockpile gradually with little fear of punishment by the international community.

A process of de-militarisation, however, would go well beyond de-nuclearisation of the Korean peninsula. It would entail eliminating North

Korea's ballistic-missile programme – probably the next negotiating priority on the security front – in large part because of the immediate, direct threat it poses to Japan, but also because of the more long-term threat it may present to the United States. Such negotiations may also be accompanied by attempts to bring Pyongyang into international regimes prohibiting chemical weapons and governing biological weapons. De-militarisation would entail replacing the current five-decade-long armistice ending the Korean War with a more permanent peace arrangement. Accompanying such an effort would be negotiations to reduce conventional forces on the peninsula. The end result, hopefully, would be a new and much more stable security environment on the Korean peninsula.

For de-militarisation to have a chance of success, it will need to be accompanied by other negotiating tracks designed to improve the political situation on the peninsula. Crucially, political and economic relations between North Korea on the one hand and the United States and Japan on the other, will have to be normalised. Such a process can be built into any Six Party Talks agreement – particularly normalisation with the United States – by demanding the establishment of diplomatic relations and the ending of all economic sanctions. Normalisation with Tokyo will require the acceleration of bilateral discussions with North Korea to resolve thorny issues such as the abduction of Japanese citizens by the North. A second track, concerning the modernisation of the Korean peninsula, will require the provision of economic assistance to Pyongyang, through international financial institutions or bilaterally, designed to improve its civilian economy and to help with economic reform. Once again, such assistance could be built into a diplomatic settlement at the Six Party Talks although separate initiatives will also be possible, internationally or bilaterally, for example through increased South Korean help for the North.

Finally, a process concerned with human-rights and human-security issues would be needed. This would address key issues such as human rights in the North, as well as the questions surrounding Japanese abductees and South Koreans who are missing and believed to be in the North. Some of these issues, such as the issue of Japanese abductees, will have to be resolved for other tracks to move forward. But, in general, there should not be a tight linkage between work in this area and other tracks, particularly de-militarisation, in recognition of the core security interests involved in this issue. In any case, the North Koreans certainly recognise that dealing with these problems is essential for the normalisation of relations with Japan and will be necessary if engagement is renewed with Western governments.[16]

NOTES

Introduction

[1] In many respects, this is the same approach Seoul has taken towards the North for many years, going back to the Roh Tae Woo administration in the early 1990s – combining economic and diplomatic approaches towards the North, in the hope that the two would build on each other.

[2] Choong-Yong Ahn, ed., *North Korea Development Report 2002–2003* (Seoul: Korea Institute for International Economic Policy, 2003), p. 24.

[3] Charles Wolf, Jr and Kamil Akramov, *North Korean Paradoxes: Circumstances, Costs, and Consequences of Korean Unification* (Santa Monica, CA: RAND, 2005), p. 14.

[4] Kongdan Oh and Ralph C. Hassig, *North Korea Through the Looking Glass* (Washington DC: Brookings Institution Press, 2000), pp. 66–7.

Chapter One

[1] For example, see Ri Dong Gu, 'Some Thoughts on the Adjustment of Farmers' Market Prices', *Kim Il Sung University Gazette*, vol. 44, no. 3, 1998, cited in Selig S. Harrison, *Korean Endgame* (Princeton, NJ: Princeton University Press, 2002), p. 41.

Chapter Two

[1] The Cold War International History Project (CWIHP) has collected documents from Soviet and East European embassies in Pyongyang. These are as fascinating to read as they are valuable, but they need to be approached with caution. Embassy observers are not always right and sometimes they are as concerned about how reporting might affect their career prospects as they are about accuracy. Woodrow Wilson Center, 'New Evidence on North Korea', *The Cold War International History Project Bulletin*, no. 14–15, Winter 2003–Spring 2004: http://www.wilsoncenter.org/index.cfm?topic_id=1409&fuseaction=topics.home.

[2] CWIHP, Document no. 9, Report, Embassy of the Hungarian People's Republic in the DPRK to the Ministry of Foreign Affairs of Hungary, 16 March 1961, pp. 83–4. See also CWIHP, Document no. 34, Report, Embassy of Hungary in North Korea to the Hungarian Foreign Ministry, 30 December 1960, pp. 131–2.

3   CWIHP, Document no. 7, Stenographic record of conversation between Erich Hönecker and Kim Il Sung, 30 May 1984, p. 57.

4   Bradley K. Martin, *Under the Loving Care of the Fatherly Leader: North Korea and the Kim Dynasty* (New York: St Martin's Press, 2004), pp. 504–5.

Chapter Three

1   The importance of understanding the political process of reform and not just the economic results of specific reform measures themselves is well illustrated in Joseph Fewsmith, *Dilemmas of Reform in China: Political Conflict and Economic Debate* (New York: M.E. Sharpe, 1994).

2   Cho Chang Dok's remarks particularly emphasised the importance of the North's energy needs and implied that these could be satisfied, in part, from direct cooperation with South Korea. This new line had immediate implications for North–South relations and for the negotiations leading to the June 2000 Inter-Korean Summit. At the same time, it also had implications for US–DPRK negotiations. With an emphasis on the economy, the diplomatic calculus changed and improved ties with both Seoul and Washington became not only possible, but even imperative. For example, the North's oft-voiced claim that it was due 'compensation' for what it said was late delivery of light water reactors promised in the 1994 US–DPRK Agreed Framework could now be addressed in new ways. His remarks can be found in *Pyongyang Korean Central Broadcasting Service*, Pyongyang, 3 February 2000, in Foreign Broadcast Information Service (FBIS), now part of the CIA's Open Source Center.

3   Don Oberdorfer, *The Two Koreas: a contemporary history* (New York: Basic Books, 2001), p. 441.

4   Joint editorial, 'Let Us Open a Passage of Advance in the New Century with the Spirit of Having Triumphed in the Arduous March', *Nodong Sinmun, Choson Inmungun and Ch'ongnyon Chonwi*, 1 January 2001.

5   Joint article, 'Let Us Vigorously Accelerate the Chuch'e-Oriented Socialist Cause While Holding High the Banner of Military First Politics', *Nodong Sinmun–Kulloja*, 21 December 2001.

6   Editorial board special article, 'Military First Politics is a Powerful Weapon in Our Era's Anti-imperialist Struggle', *Nodong Sinmun*, 1 April 2002.

7   *Ibid.*

8   *Ibid.*

9   *Ibid.*

10 *Ibid.*

11 The incident on 29 June, which occurred on the very eve of the formal start of the new economic measures, probably did not please Kim Jong Il. Pyongyang moved very quickly to contain the political fallout and to apologise to Seoul.

12 Kim Young Yoon and Choi Soo Young, *Understanding North Korea's Economic Reforms* (Seoul: Center for the North Korean Economy, Korea Institute for National Unification, April 2005).

13 Editorial bureau special article, 'Let Us Proceed Holding Even Higher the Banner of the Great Leader Kim Il Song's Revolutionary Idea', *Nodong Sinmun*, 31 July 2003; 'Let Us Add Luster to the Great Military First Era with the Revolutionary Military Spirit', *Nodong Sinmun*, 19 August 2003.

14 *Nodong Sinmum*, 19 August 2003.

15 Assistant Professor Shin Chin Ch'ol, 'Significance of Ensuring Balance Between Growth in Labor Productivity and Remunerations in Expanded Socialist Reproduction', *Kyongje Yongu*, 20 August 2002, pp. 9–10.

16 Hong Pyong U and Yi Un Ch'an, 'Powerful Socialist State Being Built Under the Great Military First Banner', *Nodong Sinmun*, 14 September 2002.

17 *Ibid.*

Chapter Four

1   Fewsmith, a careful observer, describes a 'lurching and discontinuous' quality to Chinese economic policy in the decade that many observers now mistakenly look back on as a steady process of reform. See Fewsmith, *Dilemmas of Reform in China*, p. 6.

2   For an explanation of the concept of *juche* see: http://www.globalsecurity.org/ military/world/dprk/juche.htm.

3   Chong Son Ch'ol, 'The Scientific Character of Our Party's Economic Policy', *Nodong Sinmun*, 5 October 2002.

4   Editorial bureau special article, 'Our Revolutionary Cause, Which Advances Along the Path that the Great Military First Ideology Points at, Is Invincible', *Nodong Sinmun*, 5 October 2002.

5   See Ruediger Frank, 'North Korea: "Gigantic Change" and a Gigantic Chance', Nautilus Institute, *Policy Forum Online*, 9 May 2003: http://nautilus. org/fora/security/0331_Frank.html; Frank, 'The End of Socialism and a Wedding Gift for the Groom? The True Meaning of the Military First Policy', Nautilus Institute, *DPRK Briefing Book*, 11 December 2003: http://www.nautilus.org/ DPRKBriefingBook/transition/Ruediger_ Socialism.html.

6   DPRK foreign ministry spokesman's statement, *Pyongyang KCNA* [in English], 25 October 2002, cited in FBIS.

7   Han Chong Min, 'The Principled Issues the Great Leader, Comrade Kim Jong Il, Has Illuminated for the Construction of an Economically Powerful Socialist State', *Kyongje Yongu*, 20 December 2002, pp. 2–4.

8   Yi Chang Hyok, 'Placing Importance on Defense Industry is an Important Demand for Economic Construction in the Military First Era', *Nodong Sinmun*, 22 January 2003.

9   'Let Us Develop the Defense Industry with Priority While Simultaneously Developing Light Industry and Agriculture', *Minju Choson*, 5 February 2003, p. 3.

10 Yi Chong Su, 'Important Demand for Building the Economy in the Military First Era', *Nodong Sinmun*, 28 February 2003, p. 2.

11 *Ibid.*

12 *Ibid.*

13 Editorial, 'Let Us Launch a Great Leap in Building Up the Economy Through a Bold Offensive', *Minju Choson*, 12 March 2003, p. 1.

14 Ch'ae Ch'ol Ryong, 'Chuch'e Idea is the Root of Military First Politics', *Nodong Sinmun*, 16 March 2003.

15 Editorial bureau special article, 'Military First Ideology is an Ever Victorious, Invincible Banner for Our Era's Cause of Independence', *Nodong Sinmun*, 21 March 2003, p. 1.

16 Editorial bureau special article, 'Military First Politics is a Precious Sword of Sure Victory for National Sovereignty', *Nodong Sinmun*, 3 April 2003.

17 Yang Sun, 'Faith is More Precious than Life', *Nodong Sinmun*, 9 May 2003.

18 Any reformer worth his salt would have to assume this was a reference to former Chinese leader Deng's comment on the colour of the cat being unimportant as long as it catches mice.

19 Kim Myong-ch'ol, 'Great Vitality of Military First Politics', *Minju Choson*, 24 May 2003.

20 *Ibid.*

21 *Pyongyang KCNA* [in English], 10 June 2003, cited in FBIS.

22 Editorial, 'The Army and People that Share the Same Ideology and Fighting Spirit are Invincible', *Nodong Sinmun*, 14 June 2003.

23 Kim Pyong Chin, 'Fundamentals in Enhancing National Strength', *Nodong Sinmun*, 16 June 2003.

24 *Ibid.*

25 *Ibid.*

26 Hwang Kyong O, 'The Study of Capitalist Re-Production', *Kyongje Yongu*, 20 August 2003, pp. 47–9.

27 Kim Pyong Chin, 'Great Banner that Vigorously Drives Construction of

a Powerful State', *Nodong Sinmun*, 8 September 2003.

28 Paek Mun Kyu, 'Great Political State that Highly Displays Invincible Might through Great Military First Politics', *Nodong Sinmun*, 14 September 2003.

29 Hong Ung Ch'ol, 'Modernization, Informatization of the National Economy and Construction of a Powerful State', *Nodong Sinmun*, 25 November 2003.

30 *Ibid.*

31 *Pyongyang Central Broadcasting Station*, 5 December 2003, cited in FBIS.

32 Editorial bureau special article, 'Let Us Glorify the Military First Era with the Gun Barrel of Ideology and Conviction as a Main Force', *Nodong Sinmun*, 22 December 2003.

33 Yi Ch'ang Hyok, 'Strengthening of Military Power is a Priority Task for the Economy-Science Front', *Nodong Sinmun*, 28 January 2004.

34 *Ibid.*

35 DPRK foreign ministry statement, *Pyongyang KCNA* [in English], 10 February 2005, cited in FBIS.

36 Dr Pak Hong Kyu, 'Validity of the Military First Era's Economic Construction Line', *Kyongje Yongu*, 10 February 2004.

37 Dr Kim Chae So, 'Socialist Economic Management that Realizes the Military First Principle', *Kyongje Yongu*, 10 February 2004.

38 *Ibid.*

39 Dr Sim Un-sim, 'Several Theoretical Issues for the Military First Era's Reproduction', *Kyongje Yongu*, 20 May 2004.

Chapter Five

1 International Crisis Group (ICG), *North Korea: Can the Iron Fist Accept the Invisible Hand?*, Asia Report no. 96, (Brussels: ICG, 25 April 2005), p. 12.

2 See, for example, 'North Korean Professor: Diversify Payment Methods for Labor', *Yonhap*, 26 December 2005, cited by FBIS. The piece reports an article in the Kim Il Sung University quarterly gazette. There have been other signs over the years that university journals may be a place where new ideas surface, possibly floated by reform elements to gauge the political atmosphere.

3 *Ibid.*, pp. 12–16.

4 Fewsmith, *Dilemmas of Reform in China*, p. 6.

5 *Ibid.*, p. 6.

6 Stephen Haggard and Marcus Noland, 'A U-turn on Reforms could Starve North Korea', *International Herald Tribune*, 22 December 2005.

7 Private communications, February 2006.

8 Kim Chi Yo'ng, 'Fatherland News', *Chosun Sinbo*, 19 October 2005.

9 Chu Hyon, 'It is an Essential Demand of the Military First Era to Achieve a Decisive Turnaround in Improving the People's Standard of Living This Year', *Kyongje Yongu*, 23 November 2005.

10 This is the most recent manifestation available. More recent articles may have been published but there is a significant time lag in the translations.

11 ICG, *North Korea: Can the Iron Fist Accept the Invisible Hand?*, p. 13.

12 Kim Bun Woong and Kim Pan Suk, *Korean Public Administration. Managing the Uneven Development* (Seoul, 1997), p. 354, as cited in K. Asmolov, 'North Korea: Stalinism, Stagnation or Creeping Reform?', *Far Eastern Affairs*, vol. 33, no. 3, 2005, pp. 22–54.

13 'North Korea's Secretive First Family', *BBC News Online*, 15 February 2006: http://news.bbc.co.uk/2/hi/asia-pacific/3203523.stm.

14 Private communications, July 2005.

15 'DPRK's Nuclear Deterrent Force', *Pyongyang KCNA*, 9 June 2003, cited in FBIS.

16 The 1994 Agreed Framework with the United States included provisions for eventual discussions of non-nuclear issues, including human rights.

RECENT **ADELPHI PAPERS** INCLUDE:

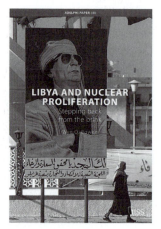

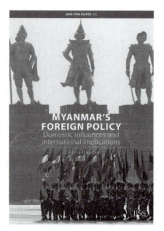

ADELPHI PAPER 380

Libya and Nuclear Proliferation

Wyn Q. Bowen

ISBN 0-415-41238-2

ADELPHI PAPER 381

Myanmar's Foreign Policy

Jürgen Haacke

ISBN 0-415-40726-5